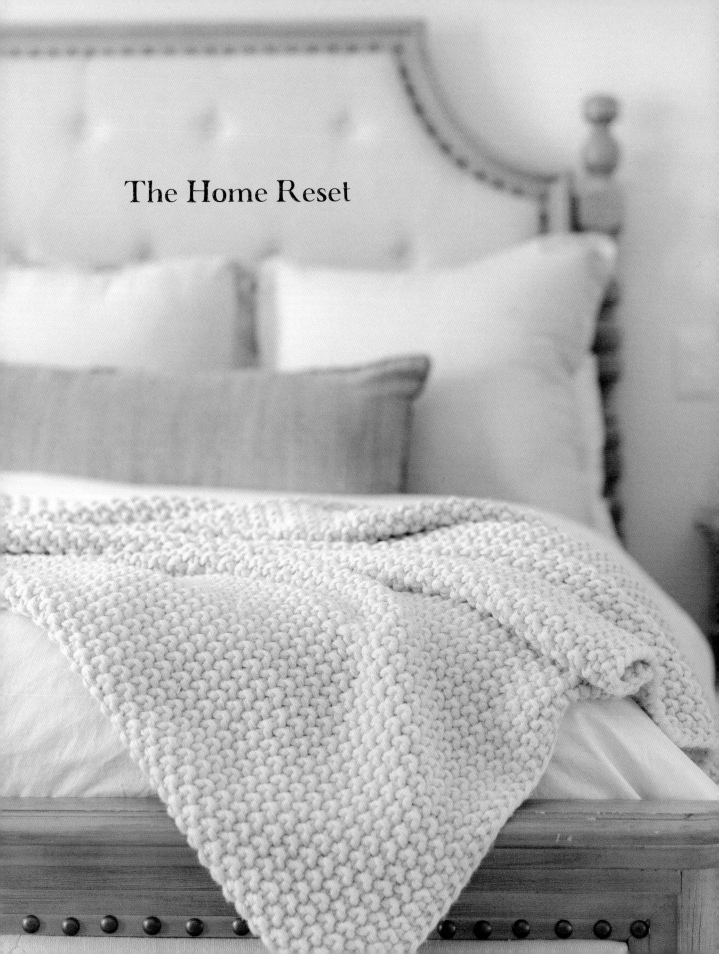

The Home Reset

Quarto.com

© 2024 Quarto Publishing Group USA Inc.
Text © 2024 Karissa Barker

First Published in 2024 by Fair Winds Press, an imprint of The Quarto Group,
100 Cummings Center, Suite 265-D, Beverly, MA 01915, USA.
T (978) 282-9590 F (978) 283-2742

Fair Winds Press titles are also available at discount for retail, wholesale, promotional, and bulk purchase. For details, contact the Special Sales Manager by email at specialsales@quarto.com or by mail at The Quarto Group, Attn: Special Sales Manager, 100 Cummings Center, Suite 265-D, Beverly, MA 01915, USA.

29 28 27 26 25   1 2 3 4 5

ISBN: 978-0-7603-8937-9

Digital edition published in 2024
eISBN: 978-0-7603-8938-6

Library of Congress Cataloging-in-Publication Data

Names: Barker, Karissa, author.
Title: The home reset : mastering systems and cultivating habits for a
   better house, condo, or apartment / Karissa Barker.
Description: Beverly, MA, USA : Fair Winds Press, 2024. | Includes index.
Identifiers: LCCN 2024016275 (print) | LCCN 2024016276 (ebook) | ISBN
   9780760389379 (hardcover) | ISBN 9780760389386 (ebook)
Subjects: LCSH: Storage in the home. | Orderliness. | House cleaning.
Classification: LCC TX309 .B36 2024 (print) | LCC TX309 (ebook) | DDC
   648/.8--dc23/eng/20240429
LC record available at https://lccn.loc.gov/2024016275
LC ebook record available at https://lccn.loc.gov/2024016276

Design and page layout: Laura Shaw Design
Photography: Oxana Brik Photography
Illustration: Shutterstock

Printed in China

The
HOME
Reset

Easy Systems & Habits to Organize Every Room

▾▾▾▾▾▾▾▾▾▾▾▾▾▾▾▾▾▾▾

KARISSA BARKER

FAIR WINDS

Contents

Introduction 6

Introduction

It can be the most wonderful feeling in the world when your home rises to meet you. Almost intuitively, it knows what you need and when: lamplight and your favorite book on a rainy day, or a warm breeze blowing in through open windows at the start of spring. Home is a place to land, a place to hold you, and a place to launch you into the world. "Home" can be a lot of things, but it takes intentionality to help it live up to all we need it for in the world.

I've struggled with chronic illness for most of my life. Home has always been a sanctuary for me, even when forced to be there and away from normal teenage life. I didn't realize until I had grown up how incredibly fortunate I had been to have home and family life as a sanctuary—and the daily small (and large) habits and work my parents put into the rhythm of life to make it a safe, comfortable space.

As an adult, I struggled to find the feeling of calm and peace that can accompany a well-ordered and clean home. I realized how little I paid attention to my mom's actual habits—the things that kept our home that way. I knew how to do things like laundry, cooking, cleaning. But doing the things wasn't the main issue. It was fitting them into a full life of motherhood and work.

When my firstborn was one-and-a-half years old, my health became extremely poor and I had to quit my job. My husband was working long hours as a pastor, and my mom took an entire year off work to be home with me to take care of my daughter while my husband was at work. She did everything to make our house feel as much like a home at that time as possible while we tried to figure out how to pay medical bills and find doctors that would help me become a person again.

As I slowly began to improve and be able to function (e.g., walk on my own, do simple tasks), my home "sanctuary" began to feel more like a prison. I went weeks without leaving

the house, and my days felt like a constant battle in trying to be "okay" while struggling to take care of the house I felt stuck in.

I began to realize that home was where I would spend the majority of my time whether I liked it or not. It needed to feel like that "place to hold you," not a place of constant overwhelm. With great reluctance, it also dawned on me that life would never go back to "before." I might never have a fully functioning body. Doing normal things would always be harder. So, I gave myself permission to try to do things outside of the "normal" way.

I began finding ways to care for my house that worked with the way I thought and the physical ability I had in that moment. The rigid schedules with divvied up daily tasks I had printed off Pinterest finally got tossed. I was ready to acknowledge that it was okay that they didn't work for me, and it was better to stop trying to make them work. New rhythms, habits, and hacks were incorporated into my day. My house became more manageable. It was more of a home than ever.

If you stop by my house on any given day, I can't promise it will be picture-perfect for your visit. Over the years, I've realized that's not the point (at least for me). Admittedly, if your visit coincided with a bad health week, my house may even be a bit of a disaster. Yet I do think keeping home has grown into something more meaningful for me. Now I don't feel like I'm constantly serving my home or the things in it. My home serves me. Things have a spot to belong in. We are not overwhelmed by "stuff." I have systems to reset each room, with my favorite cleaning tools and hacks on standby, easily accessible. We have instilled habits and routines in our family that make today's "disaster" of a house look like what we called "clean" years ago.

My hope for you, reader, is that you, too, can find the tools to change the way you live in your home. An inspirational pep talk or a photo of a clean closet may serve in the short term, but I sincerely wish for you to be able to utilize the habits and systems in this book to better your daily life long-term. Nothing in this book is intended to add to your daily load: I know you have enough on your plate as is. Every word is dedicated to an easier, more simplified and calm life in your home. Use this book accordingly. Make it your own, and adapt everything to what works for you.

May this book bless you with a reminder that the mundanity of domestic tasks may not seem like it, but they have eternal impact. You caring for your home is such a beautiful way to serve yourself and your family. Keeping house is rarely easy work, and not often enough rewarding. I see you. I'm proud of you. And I'm with you. Now let's reset your home.

1.

Success in Systems

▲ ▲

With the amount of information we have access to and all the helpful gadgets we can get our hands on, it's baffling how difficult keeping a house in order can be at times. Despite the new bathroom scrubber promising to wipe all the grime away in one fell swoop, or the vacuum that will clean dirt, mop, steam, do the laundry, and raise your kids, it still feels like an uphill battle every day. Does this ring true for you too?

You can't convince me that modern adults haven't been dealt the short end of the (broom) stick when it comes to keeping home. The modern generation didn't get a home-economics experience but instead are inundated with every possible solution to every possible problem—often for problems they didn't even know they had. You know, because they didn't take home economics. All these gadgets and suggestions add up to is more of the feeling that you are "doing it wrong" or missing something.

A lot of things changed for me when I realized that I was missing something. I may have bought all the cleaning and tidying things and learned how to use them, but my home constantly felt disorganized and messy. The reason was simply that the daily rhythm and routine of my life was, well, disorganized and messy. I didn't have systems set up to make a quick pick up or room reset possible—in fact, quite the opposite.

This made trying to stick with habits that would calm the chaos instead of contributing to it feel like trying to push a semi truck up a hill. But, as it turns out, that semi was fairly easy to drive up the hill all along once I learned the gears. Sure, it took some work and trial and error to master the driver's seat, but now I don't feel like I'm using everything in me just to not get flattened by it.

I know your life is hard and messy and complicated. Mine is too—and I still get overwhelmed sometimes by the state of the kids' bathroom or the pile of laundry. I'm not writing this book as someone who has a perfect house all the time (that's not even my goal anymore), but as someone who has fought hard to figure out how to manage over the years.

This shift in my ability to keep a calmer house is most noticeable to me after a period of struggling with chronic illness. Sometimes it will knock me out for weeks at a time. Our family goes into survival mode—oftentimes this will mean my husband is a single parent (while working full time and being my caregiver), and the house gets way messier than

Your Home Reset

How to Make This Book Work for You

This book is divided into rooms (e.g., kitchen, living room, laundry, etc.). For each room in your home, there are four sections in each chapter: the reset, habits, systems, and tutorials. I walk you through how to "reset" each room and how to rework your habits and systems to keep that space serving you, instead of the other way around. Then I share some practical tutorials for each space.

Over the years I learned that what truly put me in the driver's seat when it came to caring for my home was changing my habits, reinforcing those new habits with systems built for success, and having a clear, efficient way to reset each space in my home. I was tired of being flattened. Through learning the hard way how helpful the neuroscience of habits was when it came to trying to function with chronic illness and caring for my family through some dark times, I accidentally on purpose became better at caring for my home.

normal. Because laundry and toy storage are not a priority when you are fighting to just function in the slightest.

When I go through one of these "flare ups" (and my family goes through them with me), getting the house back to our normal, calm homeostasis takes way less effort. My husband and kids are better set up to be supported while all struggling without mom and wife, and we at least have a more peaceful home in those hard times compare to how we went through them years ago.

Your house will get messy. Things will get out of order, and changes (both good and bad) will throw everything out of whack. The goal of this book is to give you the freedom to be able to live through real life without things like laundry, dirty dishes, or clutter becoming so overwhelming that your home doesn't feel like a sanctuary anymore. Your home exists to serve you—and with a few simple changes, caring for your house goes from semi-truck heaving to more peaceful coasting.

In this chapter I will set the framework for the resets, habits, and systems in the following chapters, along with sharing my cleaning arsenal and how I set up my home to make it easier to maintain. Everything is meant to be either used as is or customized to fit your lifestyle and needs.

The Resets

Based on the nature of this book, one would think that I love cleaning. While I admittedly do enjoy a good steam mop session and the satisfaction of smudge-free glass, I absolutely do not love cleaning. In fact, I have spent a fair amount of my life thinking of ways to make cleaning my house as simple, quick, and effective as possible so I don't have to do it a minute longer than necessary.

The Reset section in each chapter is the fruit of that labor. Each room has a checklist that goes through every step of cleaning or "resetting" the space. I have done my best to eliminate redundancies, wastes of time, and distractions in these checklists. The order of each reset is what makes sense to me—adapt it to what makes sense to you. You will notice a few consistencies in the "flow" of each reset that will instantly save you time and effort:

- **Top to bottom:** Each room reset prompts you to begin at the "top" of the room and move down. Essentially this means starting closest to the ceiling and working your way down, finishing with the floor. This is an important habit to fall into when you are cleaning, and it will eliminate time-suckers (e.g., finishing sweeping the floor and realizing the kitchen table still needs wiped down, and having to sweep again when the table is done). Dust also settles downward, so wiping down tall furniture, mirrors, or light fixtures from tallest to shortest will mean everything only has to be dusted once.

- **Left to right:** This was a tip I read in a blog post written by a professional housekeeper. Each reset suggests cleaning the room from left to right, or clockwise. This tip has been

a lifesaver to me when the kitchen gets out of hand. Beginning at one side of the room and moving around it helps break up the whole reset into less intimidating sections. It also keeps you on track: If you get distracted by something, you can easily head back to where you left off, and you always know where to clean next.

- **Germ and gunk control:** You may notice, especially in the bathroom chapter, that the steps in each reset are designed not to spread germs or leave gunk on already cleaned spaces. Tips like clearing countertops left to right in the kitchen while putting dirty dishes in the sink to complete later are designed for this purpose. You can thank my degree in dental hygiene and the terrifying and incredibly strict way the professors taught us infection-control procedures. At the very least, this tendency toward type-A bacteria management will make your resets more efficient.

There are some steps to a reset you may want to add in based on your space. Each reset checklist is designed to cover all the bases for the most amount of people. So, for example, you may have a sitting area with bookshelves in your master bedroom that you'd include in your room reset with steps that aren't listed in this book. Of course, add in your own steps and let us live vicariously through you sipping tea as you snuggle in to your sitting area in your room.

Use the resets as your own or as a starting point to figure out a way to clean each room that makes sense to you. I have each of my resets printed and keep them in a dry erase sleeve so I can check off the list as I clean the room to keep me on track. This is also a helpful tip for getting the whole family on board. Keeping a reset checklist in each room (or with the cleaning caddy, which I'll introduce at the end of this chapter) means everyone is on the same page and the work can be more divided.

The Habits

The Habits section is a practical guide to incorporating habits in your everyday life that make keeping home easier. As I mentioned, over the years I have taken special interest in the research behind the neuroscience of habits and have learned to apply this knowledge to all areas of life, including keeping my home tidier.

Throughout all the books I read on habits that have shaped the way I live (some of my favorites are listed in the Resources section at the back of the book), I noticed a pattern based around psychologist B. F. Skinner's operant conditioning theory language of "stimulus, response, reward": Habits stick when you can incorporate some type of signal that prompts the habit, followed by a way to feel satisfied by a job well done.

I noticed when I started to incorporate these signals in my daily homemaking routine (e.g., kids sitting down for homeschool, time to start the laundry), and then lean in to the fulfillment of having done something positive or reward myself after completing the habit (e.g., coffee after laundry is started), it felt like less of an uphill battle to form new helpful habits.

Often in the Habits section in each chapter I will give examples for habit prompts and rewards designed to keep each room tidier and better organized. I have seen how utilizing this idea to cement helpful habits has been incredibly beneficial to my family over the years. In each room, I walk through the habits we have incorporated into our days to keep our homelife running more smoothly.

The power of positive habits in keeping house lies in the simple truth that small tweaks in daily life can lead to massive results. An example from the bathroom chapter: When brushing your teeth at night, fall into the habit of clearing your bathroom counter. The prompt and reward are already built into this habit so it's easy to begin and stick with. Your bathroom will stay cleaner, you'll be able to find the exact makeup brush you need right away, and resetting your bathroom will be so much easier and faster.

Use exactly what I wrote or use my ideas to design habit loops that make more sense for your home and stage of life. I have found that with habits, starting small and simple, rather than trying to change a bunch of habits at once, makes for better results over time. Change a tiny habit and only focus on that for as long as you need. As the habits stick and build on each other over time, you will notice that other parts of the house stay cleaner as well.

Habit-Hack Your Kids

My first trial in experimenting with the "reward" reinforcer in the habit cascade was with my daughter. I decided to hack the routine of asking her to clean up her room, her feeling overwhelmed, and then having the whole thing be a huge deal that was more difficult than necessary. This routine was so not working for us, so I decided it was time for a hack.

My daughter corresponded regularly with the fairies that lived in the woods behind our house. One day, Fern the Fairy left a note along with a spray bottle labeled "Enchanted Realm Mist." Fern explained that the fairies used it when they cleaned their houses and my daughter could use hers as well. The only catch: The mist could *only* be sprayed on a completely clean room. When used on a clean room, "splendid magic" would happen for the person misting.

I have never seen my daughter more enthusiastic about cleaning her room than after the "Council on Clean Dwellings of the Fairy Realm" left their mist. Years later, she still uses it after cleaning her room. Thankfully the fairy magic keeps the bottle constantly replenished!

Perhaps begin by choosing your biggest problem area, then immediately incorporate an easy habit from that chapter. Over time, use the positive momentum you see from that small change to add more helpful habits to your daily routine. Before you jump right in to hacking your life with habits, though, know there is one more key to success when it comes to getting homemaking habits to stick: Success is all in the systems.

The Systems

The systems I share are designed to be the framework for habits actually sticking. For example, if you are trying to stick with the habit of clearing your bathroom counter every night and you find that your drawers are disorganized and you don't know where to put stuff, then it's nearly impossible to stick with it. The systems I share will help you stay organized, make resetting rooms easier, and make building habits attainable.

You will notice a lot of the tips and suggestions in Systems sections focus on storage and organization. Don't think of this as a book on organization: Those books have been written, and I've bought my fair share of them. It turns out that pictures of organized spaces or how to perfectly store towels in a closet are inspiring—but they will not make you more organized. They'll make you *want to be*, but to get there, you have to have your habits in place with systems to back it up.

The Systems sections are less about getting a color-coded, Pinterest-worthy closet pic. (Although the pictures in this book are swoon-worthy; we have my amazing photographer Oxana and publishing team to thank for that.) The focus here is more about finding ways to support you in the habits that make life easier. I have noticed that proximity is a huge factor in a system being successful in supporting a habit. For example, we moved into a new-to-us house and jumped right into a remodel. My cleaning caddy got banished to a hall closet. That cleaning caddy fell into the no-man's-land called "out of sight, out of mind," and it also added multiple extra steps (both literal and figurative) to clean the bathrooms or anything else for that matter.

When we finished the remodel, it became easier to keep up with the habits because my cleaning supplies were close to where they were needed. You'll find through each chapter that by looking at your systems as the foundation to build your habits on, eventually the picture-worthy organization (if that's your thing) will become a new baseline. Because we've all spent three days cleaning out and organizing bathroom vanity drawers only to have them be a disaster again the next week. That's the beauty of the symbiosis of habits and systems.

The Tutorials

The tutorials are the supporting roles of each chapter. I share the nitty-gritty details of how to clean difficult things, recipes for DIY cleaning products, or further information on concepts covered in the chapters. All the practical tips found in the tutorials are designed to be affordable, attainable, and simple.

   Throughout the book you will find the tutorials at the very end of the chapters. I tend to lean toward all-natural and scent-free cleaning products, so my recipes reflect that. As with every other aspect of the book, make the tutorials your own!

Let's Get You Set Up

Use these lists to get yourself set up to fully reset your home and start living differently, and as a jumping-off point to make your own systems.

Karissa's Cleaning Arsenal

These are items I always have on hand to clean everything in my house. Over the years I have simplified what I keep on hand. I tend toward products that are multiuse, scent-free, natural, and hardworking. I also included where I keep each product. I am a person who appreciates examples of minute details, so learning where I store each thing may be especially helpful to some.

- **All-purpose spray:** Kept in the kitchen for counters and in cleaning caddy. Find my recipe for this cleaner on page 45.

- **Disinfecting spray:** Kept in bathroom vanities.

- **Disinfecting wipes:** Kept in cleaning caddy and under the kitchen sink. Use for bacteria-laden messes (e.g., raw meat juice, toilet cleaning, etc.).

- **Dish soap:** Kept in the kitchen but useful for things besides dishes as well (e.g., grease stains or spills).

- **Castile soap:** I buy in bulk and keep in my cleaning caddy and the laundry room. Can be used to mop floors, remove soap residue, or replace body wash, hand soap, or dish soap.

- **Baking soda:** In a shaker bottle (recycled Parmesan shaker to be exact) in the cleaning caddy and the laundry room. Great for scrubbing baths and showers and freshening up laundry in the washing machine.

- **Distilled white vinegar:** I keep vinegar in the laundry room to use when washing clothes, as well as in my DIY All-Purpose Spray.

- **Cleaning towels and rags:** Kept in the kitchen, cleaning caddy, and linen closet. I prefer to use them over paper towels—they clean better and can be reused.

- **Roll of trash bags:** I keep a small roll in my cleaning caddy to replace bathroom trash cans, and my large kitchen roll under the sink.

- **Melamine sponge:** Keep one in the cleaning caddy and always have a backup. These will save you in a pinch (like toddler writing on the walls or a stubborn stain in a porcelain sink).

- **Scrub brush:** Kept in my cleaning caddy. Very helpful for scrubbing grout in bathrooms.

- **Wet mop:** Kept under the utility sink in the laundry room next to vinegar and castile soap. Use on all hard floors.

- **Steam mop:** Kept in the closet. Used on tile floors. Always make sure your floors can hold up to a steam mop before using!

- **Broom and dust pan:** Kept in the laundry room right off the kitchen.

- **Upright vacuum:** Kept in an out-of-the-way closet. Used for bigger messes or jobs.

- **Stick vacuum:** Kept in the laundry room right off the kitchen. Used daily for smaller clean-up jobs.

- **Mini upholstery cleaning vacuum:** Kept in the linen closet. Used periodically for stains. This is so handy, and it makes it so much less stressful to have things like a nice rug or light-colored chair with kids.

- **Toilet bowl cleaner:** Kept on the bathroom floor tucked behind the toilet.

- **Toilet bowl brush:** Kept on the bathroom floor tucked behind the toilet.

- **Duster:** Kept in a closet with the vacuum. I tend to wipe things down with a damp cloth to dust them, but having a duster on a long handle is great for hard-to-reach places.

Karissa's Cleaning Caddy

I mention my cleaning caddy several times throughout this chapter. This is another simple system switch that can make your life so much easier. I keep a little cleaning caddy with everything I need in the bathroom. It is easy to tote around the rest of the house too. Here is how I stock my caddy:

- All-purpose spray
- Disinfecting wipes
- Baking soda shaker
- Cleaning towel

- Small roll of trash bags
- Melamine sponge
- Castile soap
- Scrub brush

2.

The Kitchen & Dining Room

My health sciences background has me thinking
through the kitchen being "the heart" of the
home through a more anatomical lens.
The heart works hard to keep the rest of the
body alive and well. The heart sets the pace:
When it isn't functioning as it should,
the whole body shuts down.

The kitchen is much the same. When you create habits and systems that work to maintain the kitchen's ability to be the lifeblood of the home that exists to serve you, it won't be long until you see those systems giving life to the rest of your home and the way your family lives in it.

You already have kitchen habits. Sometimes all it takes is switching the habits we already have engrained in our day for more helpful ones. Sure, it's nice to set your coffee mug in the sink, but could you make that habit more helpful for future you? Maybe you already have a routine of finishing the dishes at the end of the day, but oftentimes you are so exhausted that you leave them for the morning, which means not having your travel mug clean and ready for work.

Once you see your habits as working for or against you, and the systems in a room as either greasing the gears of the habit machine or throwing a wrench in them, it starts to become easier to make the switch to helpful habits and successful systems. In this chapter I'll walk you through some rhythms and habits that will keep your kitchen setting a peaceful, organized place for the rest of your home and for your life.

THE KITCHEN
Reset

STEP ONE. Clear the counters. Move left to right (clockwise) around the kitchen, putting food in the fridge, trash in the bin, and cleared plates in the sink soaking in hot soapy water. If there are things that don't belong in the kitchen or on the counter, use the kitchen table to sort that stuff into piles by room. For example, my daughter's hair tie and book go in a pile, my husband's sunglasses and earbuds in another pile, etc.

STEP TWO. Soak the range grates and begin the wipe down. Remove grates and burners from the range and hood filter above it and get them soaking in hot soapy water. If your microwave is above your range, the filter is in the bottom of it. Spray the kitchen counters with counter cleaner or disinfectant; wipe them down in the same clockwise pattern as you cleared the counters in step one. Wipe down cabinets and handles, backsplash, and baseboards as needed, from top to bottom.

STEP THREE. Do the dishes. If the dishwasher is clean, empty it. Take the silverware holder out of the dishwasher, set it next to the sink, and fill it as you load the dirty dishes in the dishwasher.

  If you don't have a dishwasher, lay the dishes and silverware to dry next to the sink as you wash. Dry anything washed by hand and put the dishes away, then scrub the sink. (See step four before you do this.) Put ice cubes, a disposal pod, or lemon peels in the disposal and run it. Put the dish scrubber away and wipe down the faucet. Dry the counter around the sink.

STEP FOUR. Clean the stovetop and oven. If the stovetop grates and burners need a soak, throw them in the sink with hot soapy water after the dishes are done (but before you wipe down the sink). Spray cleaner inside the oven and let it sit while you remove the burners, grates, and knobs and wipe down along with the stovetop. Scrub the oven and reassemble the stovetop.

STEP FIVE. Clean the fridge and appliances. Fill a microwave-safe bowl halfway with water and microwave for three to four minutes. Wipe down the fridge exterior. When it's ready, remove the bowl from the microwave and wipe down the interior of the microwave and then the exterior. Remove the dishwasher filter and rinse it. Then put it back and wipe down the dishwasher exterior.

STEP SIX. Wipe down the windows, sills, walls, and doors as needed.

STEP SEVEN. Tidy any odds and ends. This is the time to put the "piles" from step one away where they belong. Wipe down the kitchen table and chairs along with any other furniture (e.g., high chair, hutch, etc.). Throw the kitchen rags in the washing machine.

STEP EIGHT. Clean the floors. Pick up any rugs and beat them outside. Sweep or vacuum the kitchen floors. Mop the floors. When they are dry, reset the rugs.

The Quick Kitchen
Reset

- ○ **Step One**
  Clear the counters and wipe them down.

- ○ **Step Two**
  Do the dishes.

- ○ **Step Three**
  Spot clean the appliances.

- ○ **Step Four**
  Vacuum or sweep.

The Nightly Kitchen
Reset

- ○ **Step One**
  Clear and wipe down the counters.

- ○ **Step Two**
  Do the dishes.

- ○ **Step Three**
  Wipe down the stovetop and spot clean the appliances.

- ○ **Step Four**
  Clear and wipe down the kitchen table.

- ○ **Step Five**
  Sweep the floor.

- ○ **Step Six**
  Take out the garbage and replace the bag.

- ○ **Step Seven**
  Put dirty kitchen towels or rags in the wash.

- ○ **Step Eight**
  Turn off the lights.

A Note from My Kitchen

My husband is a chef and pitmaster who can destroy a kitchen like no other. Now, I've been known to create a floury mess when baking, but Colin has a special gift that often involves leaving smoky smells and bacon grease in his wake. This means the kitchen has always been one of the most overwhelming places to me to reset. But I have a feeling we all share a small part in that dread of seeing a dirty kitchen and not knowing where to start when it's time to clean.

One of the biggest obstacles when tackling a kitchen reset is how many different ways you need to clean this space: You often have to clear clutter, disinfect surfaces, wash dishes, clear plates, and the list goes on. At best, it's a lot of steps. At worst, it's a recipe for sensory overload.

After years of cleaning up behind catering order messes and baby food splatter, I found a system that works for me to reset the kitchen. I designed the reset through trial and error, so now I can look at my utterly destroyed kitchen and know where to start and how to keep going. Many of the lessons are easy to apply no matter your level of mess.

The Habits

I am a founding member of The Clean Sink Club. I have a varsity jacket on order and special dish gloves with the club name. Okay, not really. But I do have a clean sink when I go to bed at night and a little more peace of mind when I wake up in the morning knowing that to be true. (Although I may have to pursue that jacket idea . . .)

Years ago, I accidentally founded the club when a family member dropped by unexpectedly and (I'm sure on accident) gave my sink overflowing with dishes a disgusted look. I was already embarrassed about the state of my house when I opened the door to the surprise visitor, but that feeling of shame when they looked at my dirty dishes made me feel like the scum of the earth.

I can remember looking at them leaning against my counter, then looking at my dirty dishes spilling out of the sink onto the counter, and thinking "I never want to feel like this again." I decided that every day all my dishes would get done, and most every day since I have gone to bed with a clean sink.

Now I know that shame is not a healthy motivating factor, and I wish I could go back and tell my much younger working-mom-trying-to-figure-things-out self that a look of disgust from a (I'm sure) well-meaning visitor to my messy house does not mean I'm a disgusting person. These days I would tell myself it's okay to not want a messy house all the time, but self-loathing is not the driving factor that will change things—it's your habits. And then I'd give myself a cupcake from the bakery down the road that has yet to open.

If the kitchen is the heart of the home and if your habits are what shape your days, it makes so much sense to ingrain daily habits that make your kitchen a pleasant, peaceful place to be. You don't have to be motivated by shame: All a messy kitchen means is you fed yourself and the family. In fact, once you instill these habits into your routine, you don't have to be motivated at all. It's just what you do. You'll keep your kitchen in order most of the time, if not all of the time.

It all starts when we wash dishes and dry them or put them in the dishwasher. Every night we go to bed with all the dishes done, and in the morning we unload the dishwasher so it is ready to fill throughout the day.

- **Habit Prompt:** We clear the table after dinner, and we wash dishes before moving on. We start the dishwasher before we turn the lights out to go to bed.

- **Reward:** Seeing the clean sink before bed, knowing you did something for your future self.

When we master this habit, we stack it with the next one:
We go to bed with counters cleared and wiped down and with the floors swept.

When we master this habit, we stack it with the next one:
We go to bed with the appliances wiped down and the kitchen table cleared.

The Systems

The systems you utilize in your kitchen are so instrumental in sticking to the habits that make your kitchen a lovely place in which to cook and eat. The kitchen is one of the hardest working rooms in the house, so if your systems are clunky, it will feel like you always have this extra friction every time you try to incorporate new habits.

Go with the Flow

Most kitchens are set up in a "work triangle" where the sink, refrigerator, and stove form the key points. This design creates an efficient workflow in the kitchen. When you set up systems that go with the flow (layout) of your kitchen, cooking and cleaning both become easier.

Keep any "tools" in the kitchen next to the part of the work triangle where they make the most sense and create the most flow. For example, dishes, utensils, and glasses make the most sense closest to the dishwasher, in my opinion. This creates an easy flow when putting away clean dishes. It makes sense to prioritize storage space for pots, pans, and cooking sheets close to the oven.

Decide If You Are a Counter Person

I'm going to come right out and say it: You need to decide right now whether you are a kitchen counter person or not, and you need to stick to it. I am not a kitchen counter person, by which I mean I hate seeing things on my counters. I hate cleaning around things that are on my counter, and my husband and I hate cooking *around* things that are on the counter.

This means I have to create systems that allow me to hide things that end up on the counter or would often belong on the countertop, such as small appliances. Whether you tend to like a counter space that is always clear or you benefit more from having all your most used kitchen items out at all times, here are some tips to help your kitchen run more smoothly:

For Cleared Counters
- **Minimize what you keep out:** Reserve counter space only for daily-use items that are cumbersome to put away (e.g., toaster, coffee maker, or a utensil holder next to the stove).

- **Store with intention:** Think outside of the box when planning and using storage systems to clear counter clutter. For example, keep your coffee filter and coffee in the cupboard above or below the coffee maker so they are accessible and it is less tempting to leave them out.

- **Wrangle similar items together:** For chaos-free storage on your countertop, find a pretty vase or crock to store your wooden spoons and cooking utensils together. Get a mug tree to hang all your mugs on next to the coffee maker. Keep your items easy to access, but create room to utilize counter space too.

- **Store upward:** Perch your salt and pepper on top of a cake plate to free up more counter space. Use removable wall hooks or hang a pretty brass rail to keep things off the counter but hung within view and easy reach.

Fall in Love with Bins

Okay, *love* may be a strong word, but once you utilize storage bins in your kitchen systems, you'll fall into a committed *like* at the very least. Using clear storage bins for food in the pantry and fridge, as well as drawer organizers, can do wonders for creating systems that reinforce the habit of putting things away in the same place every time.

I use rectangular, clear storage bins to store similar food groups in my pantry cabinet. I can slide the bin and grab things out of the back without messing up the whole cabinet. And it makes spot checking food before grocery shopping so much easier. When things are already contained it is also easier to clean out the drawers and cabinets, and I find this system keeps them cleaner longer. I even use clear bins in the fridge to group small items for easy access (e.g., bullion, pesto, jam, mustard, and other similar-sized items).

Sing a Sonnet for (Lazy) Susan

Speaking of falling in love, have you met Susan? I don't know why people call her lazy, because she will be one of the hardest working storage systems in your kitchen cupboards. I use lazy Susans in my spice cupboard, fridge, and even had them built into a corner cabinet for easy access to pots and pans.

The Dining Area

My uncle loves history and has taken the time to write out a lot of my grandfather's extraordinary life. One of the stories he likes to tell is how my grandpa was born: on the kitchen table. Not exactly a palatable thought, but a real example of how much many families use the kitchen table for activities other than eating meals.

At any given moment in the day there may be snacks on my kitchen table, most certainly there are books, a science experiment, and possibly even a toddler. Beautiful and important things happen when families eat together around the dinner table. It's proven that children whose families regularly share dinner together are less stressed, are healthier, and have higher self-esteem. Beautiful and important things also happen around the dinner table outside of eating as well: solving math problems, scribbling with crayons, and who knows what else.

Use systems and habits to keep this important area of your home usable for however it needs to serve you in the moment. When I began homeschooling my daughter, it was a struggle to share our eating space with the crafts and schoolwork and science experiments that were constantly occupying the table. We had more than a few meals where we shoved everything to the other side of the table and squeezed our plates in the open area to eat. It felt stressful and cluttered.

The system that worked for us ended up being a hutch my husband and I found at an estate sale. I labeled bins; crafts and homeschool supplies had their own spots in a hutch. Then we began the habit of putting things away when we were done with them—which was easy now because everything had a spot. Before long, my daughter would go put everything away before we moved on to the next subject without asking, because that's just what we did.

Since then, I always incorporate a piece of furniture with doors on it in our eating space—whether it is a hutch, bookcases with doors, or a cabinet. We keep board games, school supplies, serving trays, cloth napkins, and anything else we use at the table close by.

You may have to get creative with dining area systems based on your space and how you use it. My family has lived in houses that had no room for storage at all by the kitchen table as well as houses that have had a ton. Either way, it is important to figure out a system to make this space a place to serve your family well. Here are some creative solutions:

- **Make transitions easy:** If you work at the kitchen table, keep work bags or backpacks next to you while you work. Before moving on to something else, pack everything back in the bag. If you'd like, hang a hook for your bag in this area for less resistance, or make a habit of going to put your bag where it belongs before moving on. If you have room in your dining area, consider a credenza, buffet, or hutch for storage.

- **Have a table clearing routine:** When the meal is done, the table is cleared. If you have multiple children, try rotating duties (e.g., table clearer, dish washer, dish dryer) throughout the week so everyone pitches in.

- **Consider décor:** If you have to move décor out of the way every time you want to use the table or clean it, that creates resistance. Consider keeping the table clear or minimizing what you keep on the table.

The magical part about taking time to make systems in the kitchen for food and utensil storage is how much it reduces friction when tidying up or putting things away. When things have a place, it takes so much less brain power (and time) to put things away or find them when you are looking for them. When it's time to reset an overwhelming kitchen, you know exactly where the pancake mix and the kitchen scissors and the seasoning salt go.

Your systems will reinforce your habits, and pretty soon everyone in the house starts putting things where they belong and stops asking for help finding things (that were front and center but apparently invisible until a parent came along).

Habits are hard work. Often I have felt like I was assigned Hades' punishment for Sisyphus, cursed to forever roll a mountainous boulder up a hill, only for it to perpetually roll back down the hill as he neared the top. I had the best intentions and worked hard to change, but before reaching real progress found myself back where I started, with a big ol' pile of dishes waiting for me.

What changed for me is not that I suddenly had an iron will and unwavering self-discipline. The systems I created made my habits attainable. When the rest of the pasta is already sitting in its own clear bin, all of a sudden my brain couldn't comprehend just tossing the spaghetti in the pantry. When the countertops are cleared of clutter, it is so *easy* to spray and wipe them down. In fact, I'm so used to them being clear that it feels so much *better* to have them scrubbed as well.

The Tutorials

How to Clean Hard Flooring Surfaces

When we moved to our current home, I was flabbergasted when the steam mop I used on most of my hard floor surfaces at our last house stuck to the linoleum like glue. It was probably comical watching me angrily try to clean the floor in our kitchen with the steam mop getting stuck every two inches. Using the right tool for the job makes cleaning floors easier, and avoids ruining your flooring. Here's a guide to cleaning each type of hard flooring surface most commonly found in kitchens:

- **Linoleum:** Linoleum floors can take moisture, so a regular mop is my weapon of choice for destroying dirt. My favorite combo on linoleum is steaming hot water, my magical mop mixture (page 44), and a spin mop. For stains or stuck-on dirt, use a scrub brush and the mop mixture.

- **LVP (vinyl plank flooring):** If possible, check and make sure your LVP can handle heat and moisture. Some LVP flooring can handle neither, and if that is the case, a spray mop will work well for you. If your flooring can handle heat, a steam mop is another great option. If using a regular wet mop, be cautious and make sure it is damp, not soaking wet; never leave standing water on the floor. For stains, do not use abrasive cleaners or scrubbers. Stick with a cloth and scrub by hand or a scrub brush that isn't too abrasive.

- **Hard Wood:** Similar to LVP, you never want to leave standing water on hard wood. Use a damp mop or spray mop, never soaking. Also be cautious with abrasives.

- **Stone:** If the stone flooring is sealed, clean it however you want! I preferred a steam mop on the stone floors in our last house. It did wonders for lifting dirt out of the natural variations in the stone texture. For cleaning grout lines, see tips for tile floors below.

- **Tile:** Tile floors can take most any method of cleaning. I usually use a steam mop or wet mop. The steam mop helps lift dirt and stains off grout. If your grout is in need of some TLC, use a scrub brush and baking soda mixed with water to scrub off the grime.

KARISSA'S MAGICAL MOP MIXTURE

Vinegar is a natural disinfectant and an excellent stain remover, and the castile soap lifts grime well. I love this combination because it cleans well and doesn't leave any sticky, streaky residue on the floor. It is also inexpensive and easy to buy vinegar and castile soap in bulk.

1 gallon (3.8 L) steaming hot water
1 cup (235 ml) distilled vinegar
2 tablespoons (30 ml) castile soap (scented, if you prefer)

Mix everything together in a mop bucket. Use while the water is hot, and be sure your mop is wet but not enough to leave pools of water on your floor.

How I Clean My Counters

If anyone would have told me how much time I would spend perpetually cleaning countertops over the years, I would have perfected and simplified it much earlier on. These are my go-to tips to streamline countertop cleaning:

- **The spray and leave:** I spray my countertops down, then leave them for five minutes before wiping them. This gives the counter-top cleaner time to work and will make it easier to wipe down the counters.

- **The cast-iron scraper:** This is my secret countertop weapon. I have a hard plastic cast-iron scraper that works wonders for scraping sticky gunk off the countertop without causing damage. When I find a spot that won't wipe up, I scrape it and then wipe. Works wonders!

- **The sudsy fix:** Dish soap can work wonders on oily or dirty countertops. A wet rag with a squirt of dish soap can make cleaning countertops an easy task. Make sure to wipe down counters again with just water afterward to remove any soap residue.

MAKE IT N' SPRAY IT ALL-PURPOSE SPRAY

Vinegar is a natural disinfectant and deodorizer, but don't worry, it won't leave its signature smell lingering in your kitchen. Use an essential oil of your choice to make this spray. My favorite for the kitchen is lemon. It smells so fresh and clean!

1 part distilled white vinegar
1 part water
10 drops of essential oil

Combine ingredients in a bowl and pour through a funnel into a clean spray bottle. You're ready to tackle messes!

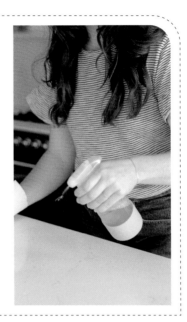

Systemize Your Sink

- **Under-sink storage:** Use lazy Susans and smart storage to keep supplies accessible and within reach.

- **Streamline supplies:** Don't keep anything under the sink that is unnecessary or you never use. Try to find cleaning supplies with more than one purpose.

- **Create a dishwashing station:** Maintain a section, either above or below the sink, with easy access to what you need to clean dishes.

3.

The Living Room

I may have accidentally established a tiny little
ego when it came to keeping my living room
tidy. We had just moved into a home that we
remodeled right as COVID lockdowns began.
The 1970s-era layout had everything divided
into separate rooms—the opposite of more
modern, airy floor plans. Between the living
room being its own space and never having
anyone over because of the pandemic, the living
room stayed pristine. I even had the audacity
to furnish it with white chairs. WHITE.

Fast-forward to our current home which is early-2000s open concept—I no longer have a problem with pride. The living room is a constant battle to keep clean. The white chairs are dangerously close to grayish. The big thing that changed is that we *use* the space now (and added in a miracle baby who is now a rambunctious toddler).

If you have an open concept home, you may know the feeling of standing in any part of your great big room and seeing allll the messes at one time. For keeping an eye on said rambunctious toddler, the space is marvelous. For not being overwhelmed by a 360-degree cacophony of life being lived and the associated mess in every living space all at once? Not so marvelous.

No matter how your home is laid out, you deserve to use your living room fully in whatever way you'd like. That's what it is there for. You just need the habits and systems in place to let it live up to its potential.

THE LIVING ROOM
Reset

Depending on your space, the living room may or may not be a straightforward room to reset. The biggest resistance to keeping the chaos at bay in my living room is all the random things that end up there and can take up a lot of time when resetting the room. In this chapter I'll show you how I have "fixed" this problem while still enjoying using the space with the systems and habits.

STEP ONE. Open the curtains and the windows. Fresh air and sunlight instantly make a room feel fresher—and they do wonders for our motivation.

STEP TWO. Dust from the top down. Dust the light fixtures, then move clockwise around the room dusting or wiping down furniture from top to bottom.

STEP THREE. Clean the windows, mirrors, doors, walls, and baseboards as needed.

STEP FOUR. Gather any items that don't belong in the room. Move around the living area clockwise collecting random items that don't belong in the living room. Place the items in piles by the living room entrance; sort them according to the room they belong in. As you go, put remotes, controllers, toys, or other "living room items" where they belong. Any dishes or kitchen things go directly to the kitchen (and if dirty, in the sink).

STEP FIVE. Straighten any remaining surfaces or areas such as shelves, pillows or blankets, and cushions.

STEP SIX. Clear the floor. Pick up anything remaining on the floor. If needed, move rugs to clean the floor.

STEP SEVEN. Vacuum the floor as well as couches and chairs.

STEP EIGHT. Mop if you have hard floors, and reset the rugs after the floor dries.

STEP NINE. Put away all the items that belong in other rooms.

The Quick Living Room
Reset

○ **Step One**
Random Roundup (see page 50)

○ **Step Two**
Straighten pillows and blankets.

○ **Step Three**
Do a quick tidy of surfaces.

Introducing the Random Roundup

I like to give care tasks fun little names. In my mind it makes the kids more excited to help, but really I'm afraid it is just because I never progressed past the third grade in executive function and I have to figure out ways to remember and make myself do things. Too honest? Perhaps. But I'll bet if you try telling yourself, "It's random roundup time!" in a game show voice, you will be more excited to pick up the day's mess.

We started the random roundup every night after dinner. I set a fifteen-minute timer, my daughter chooses fun music, and we all pick a spot in the great room (living/dining/kitchen area). For fifteen minutes we round up and put away any random items left over from the day, and my toddler follows along trying to imitate big sister. Miraculously, we go to bed with a clean living area every night. We have a fun, silly end to the night before winding down, and everyone is practicing the habits it takes to end the day (and consequently start the next day) with a clean space.

50

We set anything that belongs in bedrooms or other parts of the house on the kitchen table as we go, and at the very end we put all the random items away. A random roundup basket would be another useful (and fun) way to collect items during the roundup.

I'll refer to the random roundup in several spots in this chapter. I found that fifteen minutes is a great amount of time to start with, and when everyone pitches in, things get picked up fast.

Systemize the random roundup: The reason I love and use the room resets is that they are systems that eliminate waste—wasted time and energy in thinking through every task when resetting a space or adding in unnecessary steps. If we systemize the daily roundup too, it will make the habit so much easier to instill. Some tips to systemize the roundup:

If everyone is pitching in, everyone gets their own task: If everyone has a specific task in the roundup, it will go more smoothly. For example, "Bubba, collect all your toys and put them in your stuff spot! Sis, grab the roundup basket and find anything that doesn't belong! Daddy is going to clear the coffee table and Mama is going to straighten the pillows and blankets."

If you are doing the roundup yourself, follow the reset routine of top to bottom, left to right: Grab the roundup basket and move clockwise around the room, putting things where they belong as you go. If everything is all willy-nilly, I like to divide the room into categories (e.g., books first, then anything that doesn't belong, then coffee table, then pillows).

Stay in the living room the full fifteen minutes: This is a hack I developed to help my ADHD brain stay on task, but it is useful for everyone. Don't pick up socks and bring them to the kids' room, then come back and bring a glass to the kitchen. This is the beauty of the random roundup basket: Finish the fifteen minutes, *then* take the basket through the house, emptying it all at once.

Gather your dishes: If dishes are a constant character in the random roundup, put them all on the coffee table or a side table as you go. Bring them to the kitchen at the end of the random roundup.

Utilize the random roundup basket: Have everyone come collect their things out of the basket at the end and put the items where they belong in their rooms. If you are sick and tired of cleaning up the same toys, games, or items, maybe the items get confiscated and earned back (or maybe super stuff villain Karissa came and threw them in the trash).

The Habits

If you nail your living room tidying habits, your main living area can become a low-maintenance place of peace. Add a few low-resistance steps when you are already *in* the living room to significantly reduce your maintenance, making it a space that you look at with pleasure instead of stress. Incorporate these helpful habits throughout the day to keep the living room scaries at bay.

- **Integrate little tasks into your day:** When leaving the room, straighten pillows and blankets. Bring dishes or drinks to the kitchen when you are finished with them. It doesn't take much to stand up and straighten the pillow you just squashed before leaving the room or to drop your empty glass off in the sink as you pass by the kitchen.

- **Have a fifteen-minute random roundup and tidy every day:** Keep a basket or bin available for roundup time. Anything that doesn't belong in the living room goes in the basket to be put away in the right room.

- **Establish a weekly vacuum time:** Running a vacuum regularly over living room floors and couches keeps things looking tidier and makes full living room resets easier. It also forces you to clear the floor.

Kid Tips

Involve kids in daily cleanup time. Create a fifteen-minute Old West–style playlist and announce, "It's random roundup time!" Race to clean the living room and put random things where they belong. Make this habit your own, and find a time that fits it easily into your day. (Again, see page 50.)

Encourage kids to put their toy or book away before moving on. There will be *so much resistance*, but don't give up. Think about the life skills and habits you are ingraining in them while you remind them for the thousandth time in an hour to put their book back on the shelf before getting the blocks out. And be sure to practice what you preach. It helps me to think "don't put it down, put it away"—a great mantra from Marie Kondo that subtly reminds me of the importance of putting things away to help my present and future self.

The Systems

What is your problem? I don't mean that in an aggressive WWE-style tone. Just take a moment to think through what your *problem* is. What is the thing that makes it hard to keep your living room tidy or a place of peace? Right now for me it is toys (and spatulas, measuring cups, and anything else my toddler finds to play with and leaves in the living room). Somehow my little guy manages to not even *play* with his toys, yet they are still strewn everywhere like a tornado made its way through our home.

If there is one thing I've learned throughout my years of homemaking, it's this: If there is a problem, there's a system to solve it. That is perhaps a monumental oversimplification on my part, but systems do work. The key, however, is to overcome resistance and solve problems with your systems, not make more.

For example, I used to have a system in my living room for toy storage. I kept a nice big basket in the corner for my toddler's toys. It looked nice, had handles so it was easy to carry around and tidy up with, and was down low so my son could access it. However, the system sucked, in case you didn't catch on with the tornado analogy earlier. It was making more problems.

Here's how I solved the biggest obstacle to maintaining a peaceful living room—that basket was emptied of toys. The living room was emptied of toys. The basket formerly known as the toy bin is now my random roundup basket. I realized toys always managed to find their way into the living room, so I didn't need to help the situation out by storing them there. I also greatly reduced the amount of toys after reading some research on how much better for children a small amount or no toys is, but that's a different topic for a different day. I kept only the toys he likes to play with, and I rotate them out one at a time.

Recently I asked my followers on social media what their problem was when it came to keeping the living room tidy. By far, the most prevalent answer was kids/toys. As I read through the rest of the answers though, a common underlying theme I noticed was managing *stuff* and the people that leave the stuff everywhere: coffee table clutter, knick-knacks, dishes, laundry, pet toys. All the stuff, stuffed into the main place we all stuff in together—the living room.

Think about how much time we would save in our days if we had all the minutes back spent corralling, cleaning, and finding a home for everyone's stuff. Assuming we all don't have a desire to become nudist minimalists, we need systems that bear the weight of most of that stuff-keeping work, which is just what these systems are designed to help with.

Maintain (Far) Less Stuff

I hereby grant you the authority to get rid of the porcelain statue your mother-in-law gave you when you had your first child, and the slew of light-up, obnoxious toys the fun uncle gave your kids. If anyone asks, blame it on me. I came over and broke them. Or stole them. Or accidentally piled them up on the driveway and ran them over with my car a few times. Get creative. (I'm sure I would if I was a real-life ruthless knickknack-destroying villain.)

Your house and everything in it only exists to serve you, and I'll remind you as many times as you need. If you find yourself endlessly maintaining your stuff, it has lost its purpose and no longer serves you. Get rid of it. Here are some questions to ponder when deciding whether an item is serving you:

- **Toys:** Does your child *actually* play with it? Do they sit down and spend time with it? Or do they take it out and promptly leave it on the floor? Is there more than one toy that serves the same exact purpose? For example, why do I have four trucks on the floor in the living room when my son plays with one? Does the toy spark your child's imagination and encourage open-ended play? Is the only reason you have the toy because it was a gift and you are afraid to hurt feelings if you get rid of it?

- **Knickknacks and décor:** How do you feel when you look at the item? Why are you keeping it? Does it complement the rest of the room? Does it serve a purpose ? (Remember: Beauty is a purpose.) Do you have more than one? Do you want or need more than one? Do you truly want it? Is it worth you spending time caring for it?

- **Pillows and blankets:** How do you feel when you use the blanket? Is it pretty but also kind of scratchy or not the right size? Do you like the pillows enough to justify your time in caring for them? There is no right answer to this—only what you truly think.

A (Tough Love) Note on Gifts

When I think about it, the culture of gift-giving has gotten out of hand. Instead of noticing a need or want in someone's life and choosing to fill that need out of a generous spirit, culture has "evolved" gift-giving into an obligation that arrives incessantly.

On the receiving end of the exchange of trinkets, I find myself bearing the obligatory weigh of accepting something I do not want or need with deep gratitude. The obligation then extends to keeping and caring for the thing I do not want or need in perpetuity, displaying it in the off chance the giver stops by, and finding space for it in *my* home.

How silly is that?! It is possible that I'm letting my Ebenezer Scrooge side show, but when I think about this burden you and I place on ourselves of having to receive a gift we didn't want, act eternally grateful, and care for this thing we didn't want in our own home, it makes me so frustrated.

Be free of that. It may hurt people's feelings, on the very small chance they find out you didn't keep the things you don't want, like, or need. They may even throw a little fit if you ask not to exchange gifts for every holiday. (Do we really need "boo bags" now for Halloween?) But, those are not your feelings to manage or be responsible for. You are responsible for your feelings and for keeping *your* home a place that serves *you*.

When I took down and donated a piece of art I hung out of obligation, I felt so much better. I'm fairly certain that the person who gave it to me truly despises me, and I realized every time I looked at it I got an icky feeling and felt stressed. WHY would I keep that in MY house? Just because it is a gift does not mean you are under any obligation to keep it. And it certainly does not mean you are indebted to care for that stuff for the rest of your life. Get rid of it. Donate it, regift it, burn it, throw it off the roof, or tell them I stole it. But do not spend one more second of your life caring for a burdensome inanimate object that should only exist to serve you.

Get Creative with Storage

The living room will have your stuff in it because it has you in it. That's just the way it is, but it doesn't mean that stuff doesn't get overwhelming. Hopefully now that you've looked at the amount of stuff you have, you'll feel better about lessening your load, but there will always be stuff. So, your living room systems need to outsmart the stuff. Your biggest weapon in the living room stuff battle is furniture:

- **Have one or two designated pieces of storage furniture.** A bookshelf, cabinet, side table with storage, or coffee table with extra space underneath to hide things away are good options. You can even buy couches with hidden storage compartments!

- **What can fit nicely in that storage space is what can stay in the living room.** However, having the space does not make it a system that serves you. It's just the first step. Next, we need to figure out how to utilize it.

Cube Organizers

Is your cube organizer shelf pulling its weight or adding to yours? I know this type of shelf is popular and affordable, and it's marketed as an effective storage solution—but is it? If this is a system everyone can easily use, keep it. But if the cubes are pulled off the shelf and contents are dumped periodically throughout the day, or the books fall off the back of the shelves, or it looks cluttered even when it is "cleaned up," this may not be a system that is working in your main living space.

I know that furniture is expensive. Storage-driven pieces such as cabinets or shelves can be thrifted and made to fit your space. I ended up moving our cube shelf to the play area and opting for closed-door storage in the living room. When you need to reset a room in a hurry, being able to hide things behind doors can be useful. Even if things get messy in the cabinet, I can close the door and the living room instantly feels more put together. Doors also serve as another step between your child pulling everything out of their "stuff spot" at once. "Out of sight, out of mind" is a powerful psychological tool we can use to our advantage.

Utilize Smart Storage

After you have chosen the designated are in your living room to store stuff, use it well! This is where habits and systems meet.

- **Repetition is your friend:** When your child is prompted to put their books on the same shelf every day during random roundup, or you adopt the "don't put it down, put it away" mantra, your systems will be utilized fully and work harmoniously with your habits.

- **Give your child a "stuff spot":** They get a designated shelf or bin, and that is where their living room things belong.

- **Keep surfaces clear:** Reconsider the décor on your coffee or side table, depending on how you live in the space. Are you able to have the coffee table books and a candle stay in place and clean around them as needed? Or are they shoved to the side and repositioned? If you are serving the décor and constantly caring for it, it may not be serving its purpose well enough to keep a prime spot on the coffee table.

- **Have a battle plan for drawer space:** Utilize drawer organizers to create a system. This is where the remote goes, this space is for the current book you're reading, and this is where the flossers you always reach for go.

- **Make your space beautiful:** You have more motivation to maintain a space that is visually appealing, plain and simple. Make a small change, such as hanging a piece of art, or overhaul the entire space. Just try to make it a place that you love to look at and be in.

- **Rotate toys:** When I cleared all the toys out of the living room, I got rid of most of them, and what I did keep I separated into bins and stored high in my son's closet. I keep a few books and one or two toys in the living room and rotate them out periodically. Not only does my son play better and longer with that toy, but our whole living area stays drastically more tidy.

Reengineer Your Laundry System

Another subject that came up often in my poll was laundry. A lot of people fold laundry in the living room, which can be simultaneously convenient *and* cumbersome. If you find yourself having to move laundry to sit down in your living room, or clothes never quite find their way to where they belong, your laundry system isn't serving you.

Unfortunately, laundry is one of those household tasks that take an iron will, perseverance of habits, and an airtight system to stay on top of it. I really despise laundry, but as I do not live in a climate conducive to nudism, I must persevere in the clothes washing department. I will get into the finer details of laundry systems in chapter 7, so for now I will acknowledge it as a problem that needs a better system and offer a few quick tips:

- **Establish a laundry ritual with a beginning and an end:** This is especially important if you are a living room couch folder. Listen to a podcast, sip some tea, and fold laundry. Adding in something pleasant to look forward to while you fold is helpful. The real key, however, is the end: Fold the laundry and put it away. Keep going until that last sock is put away, and only start folding when you have the time to see it through till the bitter end.

- **Figure out a folding spot that works for you:** You don't have to do laundry the way you saw it done growing up. Heck, if there is a good reason for you to fold laundry in the shower or on the roof, have at it. Don't be afraid to try a new system for how and where you do laundry, especially if your current system makes your living area unlivable. (Again, I have so much more on this in chapter 7.)

The Tutorials

Carpet and Upholstery Care

In one of my worst-wife moments, my husband and I were painting the living room in our first house when I noticed he dripped a small amount of paint on the carpet. I chastised him for not being careful enough as I accidentally kicked over the entire bucket of dark brown paint on our brand-new carpet. It was then that I realized the power of warm water, dish soap, and a vacuum (as well as my husband's self-restraint).

I panicked. He grabbed warm soapy water and the wet/dry vac. Thirty minutes and more than a few tears later, you'd never know there was a gallon of paint dumped on the middle of the living room floor.

A compact, portable carpet cleaner is a great investment to make as a home owner. Admittedly I have spilled more paint over the years, along with too many other things to count. My clumsiness has not improved, but thankfully my preparedness has.

- **Remove a fresh stain:** Whip out your little carpet cleaner or wet/dry vac. Add 2 tablespoons (30 ml) of dish soap to a large bowl of warm water. Pour a small amount of the soapy water on the stain and let it sit for one to two minutes, then use the vacuum to suck up all of the water. If necessary, lightly scrub the stain with the soapy mixture on it with a cleaning brush. A wet/dry vac or other wet/dry vacuum will do the trick too; don't use a normal vacuum that isn't built to suck up water.

- **Remove a dry and set stain:** Mix 1 tablespoon (15 ml) of dish soap, 1 cup (235 ml) of distilled white vinegar, and 1 cup (235 ml) of water in a spray bottle. Mist the stain and blot it with a clean rag. Let it sit for ten to fifteen minutes. Wipe up with a clean, wet rag. Repeat if necessary until the stain is gone.

DIY CARPET AND UPHOLSTERY STAIN REMOVER

Mix 1 cup (235 ml) of warm water with 1 tablespoon (15 ml) of liquid dish soap.

Dip a clean, soft washcloth or rag in the mixture, then dab it on the stain.

Dampen another clean cloth with water and lightly dab and rub until the stain and soapy water are lifted. Repeat until the stain is gone.

CARPET DEODORIZER

This was a trick that I learned early on in my homemaking days from a friend battling pet odor in her carpet, and I've often used it since.

You'll need a bottle with a shaker lid: I repurpose an empty, clean Parmesan cheese bottle. Fill the bottle with baking soda and 15 to 20 drops of essential oil of your choice (My favorite is lavender; just make sure you are using an essential oil blend that is clear and will not stain). Sprinkle it on carpets and let it sit for ten to fifteen minutes, then vacuum it up. The baking soda will collect dust like a magnet and acts as a natural deodorizer and leaves carpet smelling fresh.

Dusting

For rooms with tall ceilings, get a duster on an extension pole to reach light fixtures or ceiling fans that are out of reach, or get creative by securing a cleaning rag with a rubber band to the end of a broom to dust.

To save your back when cleaning baseboards, use a clean, damp floor mop and run it around the room. I like to minimize the amount of cleaning tools I have to store, so I try to make things I already have work for multiple purposes. You can also buy a multipurpose wall and baseboard/trim cleaner on an extender.

Instead of a duster, try a damp cloth. This is my favorite way to dust. When I first began taking care of my own home, I thought I needed a cleaner for every job. Then I had to figure out how to store and clean up my cleaners. I also have noticed that a lot of the cleaners marketed as a spray to use when dusting tend to leave a residue that attracts more dust (perhaps so we need to use it more?). And many of these are full of aerosolized chemicals that I don't want in my home. A damp rag is easy to store, has many functions, can be cleaned and sanitized, and will wipe things down without leaving residue or causing damage.

A damp melamine sponge does wonders to clean dirty fingerprints off doors, walls, and light switches. It also works on crayon, pencil, scuff marks, and a myriad of other things. Just be sure not to scrub too hard or your paint will come off too!

4.

The Bedroom

▲ ▲

I loved to decorate my bedroom when I was
growing up. I'd rearrange the furniture weekly,
and my mom always obliged my (at times off-
the-wall) paint ideas. The only problem was the
constant state of disaster I kept it in. Clothes were
strewn everywhere, books were piled on every
surface, and the bed was never made. When I
felt the sudden impulse to clean or rearrange,
the only way I could think to restore order was to
remove everything from the floor (so most of my
possessions), shove them in the hall, and bring
each item in one by one and put it away.

After I grew up and got married, my household reflected the grown-up version of my kid-like tendencies toward disorganization and chaos. The only difference was the level of shame I felt as I was drowning in a sea of chaos while trying to keep the people I was responsible for afloat. As a kid, I didn't mind the swim. As an adult, I felt like I was sinking my whole family's ship.

The bedroom was the place I most felt the tension that lack of order could bring. I decorated my room like a sanctuary: calming colors, peaceful art, comfy chairs and soft fabric. Yet, there were clean clothes on a chair, dirty clothes on the floor, and piles of things to put away. I wanted the space to feel like walking into a spa, but reader, it did not.

I tried cleaning schedules, writing on the bathroom mirrors, mantras, and even hiring help in the form of professional cleaners. Still, I always returned to living in fear of someone unexpectedly dropping by, opening my master closet door, and seeing all the stuff I shoved in there to make my bedroom look presentable.

I realized the problem wasn't because I didn't clean enough. Somehow, I managed to clean and pick up constantly—and things were still a mess. I realized that the systems I had in place were contributing to chaos, and my habits reinforced them. Slowly I began to change my habits and systems, and slowly my room became a place of peace.

THE BEDROOM
Reset

STEP ONE. Open the curtains, and if you'd like, open the windows as well to let in natural light.

STEP TWO. Make your bed.

STEP THREE. Round up any dishes, glasses, or trash and take them directly to the kitchen sink and garbage. Anything else that doesn't belong in your bedroom, leave by the door until you are done with the reset.

STEP FOUR. Tidy the nightstands. Begin with the top surface of your nightstand, then move to the drawers, placing things where they belong. Wipe down the top surface of the nightstands.

STEP FIVE. Dust the room top to bottom. Make sure to dust the light fixtures and the tops of tall furniture. Wipe down the baseboards and walls as needed.

STEP SIX. Clear the dressers and furniture. Put clean clothes away where they belong, and put dirty clothes in the hamper. Tidy the surfaces, and then wipe them clean.

STEP SEVEN. Clear the floor. Pick up any remaining dirty clothes and things that don't belong on the floor and put them where they belong.

STEP EIGHT. Clean the windows and mirrors.

STEP NINE. Vacuum and/or mop.

STEP TEN. Put all the random items you left by the door away where they belong.

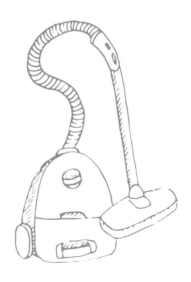

The Quick Bedroom
Reset

○ **Step One**
Make your bed.

○ **Step Two**
Put dirty clothes in the hamper and put clean clothes away.

○ **Step Three**
Clear the dresser and nightstand.

The Closet
Reset

○ **Step One**
Put all dirty clothes in the hamper.

○ **Step Two**
Collect empty hangers and hang them together in a designated spot.

○ **Step Three**
Straighten the drawers and storage, refolding items that need it.

○ **Step Four**
Put away clean clothes.

○ **Step Five**
Straighten the shoes.

○ **Step Six**
Straighten the accessories.

○ **Step Seven**
Wipe down the mirror, baseboards, and walls as needed.

○ **Step Eight**
Vacuum/clean the floors.

The Habits

My favorite thing about making my bed in the morning is that it's pretty easy, but the pay-off in seeing it made makes me feel like I did a whole day's work. It gives me the confidence of a competent person who has her stuff together. For something so small, it makes a huge difference to the start of my day. And for something so easy, it's a simple way to feel good about myself in the morning. But getting started with this routine is so hard!

Okay, you may be a bed-making rock star who has this task so ingrained in your morning routine that you don't even think about it. If so, that's amazing. What a way to start your day. On the other hand, if you, like me, suffer from a mental block when it comes to making your bed in the morning, have no fear.

Habits take away decisions, and systems take away resistance. When our morning and nighttime routine are habitualized, everything will be easier and your bedrooms will be all the better for it.

MOVING AND BAD LAUNDRY HABITS

Our most recent move and subsequent remodel made the idea of my bedroom being a sanctuary laughable for a time, but it is a prime example of how many more decisions I must make in the day when the space is not in order. One of the biggest struggles was managing our clothes, and I know this is a sticky point for a lot of people. For ten weeks we did not have a closet (or more than one small bathroom), and our room was a disaster. I found myself feeling stressed every time I entered my room, wearing the same ratty sweats over and over, and I was not sleeping well. Consider this example of habitualizing and systemizing how you care for your clothes and how many more decisions flow from it:

- When you are not in the habit of putting your laundry away immediately, you must make the decision to either look through your drawers and closet to find an outfit or go dig through the dryer or clean pile of clothes on the chair.

- When you do not have a well-working system in place to put away and store your clothes, you have to decide with every garment whether it is worth it to dig through the closet for a spare hanger to hang it up. You could also open the drawer, but half of the clothes are unfolded and you'd have to stuff the garment in—but should you fold it first even if most everything else is thrown in haphazardly? You decide to throw it on the chair with the other clean clothes, knowing you will not be able to find it easily, it will be wrinkled, and you will have to look at your chair pile of clothes before you fall asleep and as soon as you wake up. This system then reinforces the unhelpful habits above, creating more decisions, discomfort, and resistance in your day in a perpetual loop.

Morning Bedroom Habits

This is the section where I dare you to think about your bedroom habits (I'm talking about *tidying* habits, sheesh). Then look at them through the lens of eliminating unnecessary decisions, stress, and resistance in your day. Here are sanctuary-making morning habits:

Make Your Bed

I know, I know. You get it. I get it. Everybody gets it. But is your bed made today? This is where all of my reading up on habits is going to benefit you. I have realized that the main reason I don't make my bed in the morning is because I run out of it and never look back. My toddler wakes up before the sun and usually the first words out of his mouth are "More, More!" His way of saying, "Feed me mama, or I'll perish this instant or at the very least yell loudly until I'm fed!"

By the time 9 a.m. rolls around, we've been up for at least three hours. I have fed the kids, played outside, changed diapers, cleaned the kitchen and living room, played a day's worth of games, and read some board books. Usually at about this time I realize that I haven't had breakfast or coffee yet. The kids are dressed, but I'm most likely still in my pajamas. I haven't stepped foot in my bedroom all morning, and am lucky if I made it to the bathroom. (If I did, it certainly wasn't without a toddler getting in the shower fully clothed or unrolling the toilet paper.)

Now, I could tell myself "Karissa, why don't you get up earlier? Make your bed, do a little workout, shower and get dressed, and do something for *yourself* before the kids wake up!" In fact, I told myself that for years, and I've tried. Even now, every time I see a morning routine video where the mom films herself "waking up" in a matching leisure suit with brushed hair and "no makeup," I still feel like that person who can't understand why she can't just be like "that" (whatever *that* is).

But this book is for my real life, and yours too. It's not so we can have a perfect house all the time. It's so we can live in our house all the time and have it work for us.

When I suggest you create a habit of making your bed, that is all I mean. I don't mean you should be waking up at 5 a.m. before everyone else does to make your bed and do XYZ. (I swear, my kids can sense from their deep slumber when I open my eyes in the morning. I understand that waking up before your kids may not be feasible, and the frustrating experience of trying to wake up early for alone time only to have the kids wake up five minutes later every time.)

But here's the thing: I promise you that when you make your bed in the morning, it makes the rest of the day better. It begins that force of inertia toward tidiness in every other step of your day. You already made your bed first thing—of course you'll empty the dishwasher. Your bed is made at night before you get in it, and you find yourself wanting to tidy your nightstand because your bed looks so lovely. Your bed and nightstand look so inviting, you may as well grab those dirty socks and throw them in the hamper.

The bedroom is a great place to incorporate the prompt-habit-satisfaction cascade. To refresh your memory and simplify the concept: Science has shown that our habits are shaped by the signal that prompts the habit, and the reward that follows it. If we can interrupt this cycle and hack it to change our behavior, we will end up with more helpful habits.

Here's how to hack your brain at the beginning of the day by making your bed:

- **Pick a signal:** My prompt to make my bed is when I lay my youngest down for his morning nap. I announce to my oldest it is time to make beds and brush teeth, and we head to our rooms and do just that.

Some ideas for you:

» When you go to brush your teeth
» When you walk past your bed to get your clothes on
» As soon as you get out of bed in the morning

The idea of a signal is something that clicks on in your brain that says "Oh yeah! When I see/smell/hear this, I normally do that." Stick with the same prompt before your habit long enough and it'll be a part of your daily routine that you won't even have to think about.

- **Be strict with your habit:** Try to make your bed in a similar way and fashion every time. Make it easy for your brain to check out and your body to go through the motions.

- **Find a reward:** I love decorating, so seeing my bed made is a big reward for me immediately and when I walk past my room throughout the day. It may be the same for you, but if not, here are ideas to fulfill the reward part of the habit loop:

  » Grab your coffee right after making your bed.
  » Listen to a podcast while you make your bed.
  » Say an affirmation: "What a great way to start the day!" or even a "Yay me!"

Tidy Your Nightstand

Regardless of whether you have a delicious treat waiting on your nightstand before going to sleep, climbing into bed with a clean surface right next to you feels so good. So does looking at it next to your made bed when you pass by your bedroom all day.

Making your bed, clearing your dishes, and doing a quick tidy of your nightstand in the morning could all happen within a five-minute span once you nail your morning routine habits. It doesn't matter if the rest of the bedroom is a mess otherwise: Having a made bed and a tidy nightstand can make a room feel so put together that it defies the laws of science.

I have found the most success in breaking down a larger habit, like keeping my bedroom clean, into smaller habits that are concrete and tangible (and of course reinforcing with systems; more on that in the next section). I try to focus on

Do Your Dishes

If I were a heroine in a novel, this next embarrassing tidbit I'm going to tell you would be endearing instead of mortifying. So, I'll just pretend to be a main character (which involves another branch of neuroscience altogether) and forgo the embarrassment: I am a chronic bed eater. Not as in "an insatiable desire to eat cotton sheets," but as in "if I don't have a little sugary treat before bed, I don't know what to do with myself." Oftentimes I enjoy this little treat tucked into bed or in a bubble bath. Either way my dishes end up on my bedside table.

I may be the only weird person who enjoys a bedtime treat, and you may find it downright repulsive that I eat my little snack in bed, but chances are you've ended up with a water bottle or glass of water on your nightstand plenty of times (and have you tried eating frozen cookie dough sitting under a heated blanket?).

I may be Cookie Monster's nocturnal cousin, but I have enough sense to know dishes don't belong in the bedroom. Taking care of your sneaky little nighttime snack dishes in the morning is an easy habit to stack on top of making your bed. Which could be a prompt to then stack the habit of grabbing your laundry to go start a load or something else helpful.

one habit at a time, and once I notice that the habit is ingrained in my day, then I'll stack another habit on top of that one.

Usually I can tell when a habit is ingrained in my day by how consistently I respond to my prompt. Think Pavlovian conditioning. When you try to incorporate too many habits at once, there can be too much resistance to let it become routine.

Bedroom Habits throughout the Day

As I alluded to when harping on about making beds, something magical happens when your bed is made in the morning. It's like starting every day fresh with a home ready to be your place of peace.

Newton's Law of Motion definitely applies to keeping a tidy home. Once you get the ball rolling, it will stay rolling. All of a sudden when you go to automatically throw your pajamas on the floor with the other dirty clothes, you have the thought: "Don't throw your pajamas on the floor. You just picked up your nightstand and made your bed. Throw them in the hamper!" It begins to even feel *silly* not to continue to care for our bedroom, then the rest of the house.

Don't be surprised when your bedroom magically begins to stay tidier every day. No, it's not a magical cleaning fairy who shows up when you are at work—it's *you*. An object in motion stays in motion. Keep up the momentum by incorporating these habits throughout the day:

- **Put your clothes away:** Gosh darn it, put them where they belong! This is one of those big-picture habits I talked about earlier that may work better to break into smaller baby habits.

- **Dirty clothes in the hamper:** Your signal is when you take your dirty clothes off. Beat that resistance. You got this! Clean laundry gets put away immediately: "Don't put it down, put it away!" This little mantra made its way around social media a few years ago, and it has always stuck with me. I couldn't tell you how many trips I make through my bedroom throughout the day that I end up setting down something random. At the end of the day, there is a bunch of random stuff in my room that gets pushed to the side.

I like to repeat "Don't put it down, put it away" when I go to set something random down where it doesn't belong. It's the reminder that it may take ten to fifteen more seconds to put my book or claw clip away where they belong instead of tossing them on the dresser, but it is less work in the long run.

- **Trash belongs in the trash:** Find a consistent time during the day to throw away any trash in your room, or have a trash bin somewhere convenient (and subtle if you don't want to look at it). Before you tuck in for the night or when you are done getting dressed in the morning, wrangle any trash and toss it where it belongs.

The Systems

Did your eighth-grade math teacher have an inspirational poster that showed a side profile of an iceberg, with just one quarter of it sticking out of the water and most of the mass living unseen in the depths of the ocean? That's how I view the relationship between systems and habits, and that may be the only part of eighth-grade math that stuck with me.

Your habits are what you see and notice, but there are these deep systems keeping your habits afloat. When your systems get out of whack, it makes keeping your habits that much more difficult. That's why when you go on vacation you often don't maintain the habits that are normal to you—all the healthy and helpful habits are still available to you and possible, but the environment and systems are completely changed.

The bedroom may not seem like a room where systems are as important as, say, the kitchen, but they are equally significant in feeling like your home is in order. The main systems to focus on streamlining in your bedroom are intertwined with the main habits we focused on earlier.

Choose Your Own Bedding Adventure

I never once considered not using a top sheet until I learned that Europeans don't. I didn't even fact-check; I just took it as permission to take off the cumbersome thing and move on with life. That one little switch made making my bed so much easier and quicker. My husband is so tall that his feet hang off the end of the bed. Every single morning making the bed felt like starting from scratch, straightening and then tucking every single layer in.

Here's your permission to make your bed however you want. See potential bedding options on the opposite page. But I'll add in a caveat: Make it a system that works for you. If adding in six extra decorative throw pillows to the mix feels tedious, do without them. If layering pretty quilts and shams fulfills that reward part of the habit loop, find a system that eliminates resistance when you make your bed in the morning. Here are some suggestions:

- **Create a system for storing any decorative pillows or blankets:** A nighttime storage system makes it easy to make your bed in the morning, and you won't be looking at clutter before you go to sleep. Put them on a chair or bench, or in a folded pile next to your dresser.

- **Only keep bedding that is in good condition and functional:** If the pillowcases slip off the pillow every night, your duvet is starting to get a hole, or the fitted sheet doesn't quite fit your mattress, replace them. Eliminate any excess resistance or anything that detracts from a feeling of calm in your room.

- **Make your bed easily accessible:** Consider moving any furniture that is too close to the bed or that gets in the way of making it.

Fast and easy

A little more detail

All in on the throw pillows

No More Nightstand of Doom

When we were remodeling the bathroom, our bedroom was a disaster zone and my nightstand became an eyesore. Not only that, it completely ceased all function as a contributing member of the bedroom furniture family. At one point the top drawer was so loaded down with books that it wouldn't shut and the whole thing tipped over, unfortunately landing in a pool of freshly spilled grout water. My lamp shade was ruined, and I had an even bigger mess to clean up than a pile of books on the nightstand.

Visually, having a tidy nightstand creates a sense of peace and calm before bed. Functionally, having a tidy nightstand can do the same:

- **Assess whether your piece of furniture is serving you well:** If your nightstand is not meeting your needs, consider finding a different option.

- **Have a system for your drawers:** I have three drawers in my nightstand: The top drawer has pens, lip balm, my Bible, and current book I'm reading. These are things I use consistently every night. The pens and lip balm are contained in a rectangular plastic organizer closest to the bed so I can access them without having to dig through them. The second drawer has books and journals I like to look through often but not every day, as well as special notes from my husband and kids. The bottom drawer has a heating pad that I use frequently.

When creating your own drawer system:
- **Use drawer organizers:** You can buy fancy ones from a home store, or find them at a dollar store or use small boxes. Make everything you use on or in your nightstand have a designated, contained place.

- **Keep the things you reach for most the closest:** If you find yourself digging in your bottom drawer for a flosser every night, maybe they need their own spot in prime top drawer real estate.

- **Consider minimizing what you keep on the top of your nightstand:** I used to have a tray, an orchid, books, and a little trinket on my nightstand. I even put a matching orchid on my husband's (without asking). Lovely, yes. Functional? In no way, shape, or form. I'd be shoving the plant to the side, nothing fit right on the tray, and there was no spot for my little sweet treat. Now I only keep a lamp, a little picture frame, and a small clock.

Help Clothes (Finally) Find Their Way Home

Normally I subscribe to the save-the-best-for-last concept, but not this one. I saved the hardest, most treacherous, mountainous pile of laundry for the very last system to tackle. I guess that means it's all down the clean laundry hill from here.

- **Figure out folding:** Again, I give my most solemn permission for you to figure out a folding system that works for you. It doesn't have to be the way your mama or your auntie or your nana did it. In fact, if they see you folding or storing your clothes in some newfangled way and it offends them, let me know and I will send my formal condolences for leading you astray. If it causes too much resistance and is not working for you, scrap it.

- **Overhaul your laundry hamper:** Consider getting one with a lid.

- **Make an emergency plan:** Unfortunately, it doesn't work to say "under no circumstance store clean clothes anywhere other than hung up or folded away." Sometimes that chair in the corner of your room will get a sweater thrown on it. But here's the thing: That sweater attracts more buddies, and before you know it, the whole gang is camping out together on the corner blob (formerly known as the corner chair).

  Life happens. Clutter happens. Have an emergency plan system in place: When you begin to notice a chair party in the corner, aim to tackle it before it turns into an abstract art piece. Notice and acknowledge it, and plan a time (that day) to tackle it. Set a reminder on your phone or an alarm if you have to. If your executive function just isn't executive-ing, listen to a podcast or watch a show while you make yourself do it.

FOLDING STRATEGIES

Look up folding methods on YouTube and try something new: I watched a Marie Kondo video on folding and found that her method helped me save drawer space. Once I got the hang of it, it was easy and fast.

Consider not folding: GASP. I said it. This can be especially useful with kids. My big kid doesn't care to keep her clothes folded. It doesn't bother her in the slightest to look through a drawer or bin to find clothes that are all mixed together. Now, I let it happen. It used to trigger my anxiety, and I'd spend a lot of time refolding things. But that system didn't work for my daughter, and it made more work for me.

Have hangers that work: And maybe even have hangers that are a little bit pretty. When your clothes look nice hung up, you are more likely to continue to want to hang them up. This concept also works for drawer storage. If you find that opening your clothes drawer gives you anxiety, consider overhauling how you fold or store things. If you have large or deep drawers, get drawer organizers to help keep things tidy. Once you take the time to create a system that works for how you want to use your dresser or clothes storage, the habit of putting things away where they belong will more easily fall into place.

- **Assess your clothes storage system as a whole through the problem-solving lens:** Does your snuggly robe always initiate the corner chair party? (Asking for a friend . . .) Maybe you need a robe hook in the bathroom instead of expecting yourself to hang it up on a hanger every day. Does your work outfit inevitably get thrown on the floor every day when you get home and change into comfy clothes? Maybe your laundry hamper should move closer to where your comfy outfits are. What problematic patterns do you notice that create resistance in your room, and how can you fix them? Don't be afraid to think outside the box. Your closet and clothes only exist to serve you.

- **Reset your laundry system:** We aren't going to tackle this Goliath until chapter 7, but get ready friend! We've got some good stones to throw.

The Tutorials

How to Refresh Your Mattress

Remember the shaker bottle of baking soda we used as a carpet deodorizer? (See page 64.) It's an excellent tool for freshening up your mattress. Sprinkle it over your mattress and let it sit for about twenty to thirty minutes, then vacuum it off. This is a great step to do as soon as you take your sheets off to wash them. Baking soda is a natural deodorizer.

If you need to clean a stain off your mattress, mix together ⅓ cup (80 ml) of hydrogen peroxide and a few drops of dish soap. Blot the mixture on the stain with a clean rag. Let it sit for three to four minutes, then blot the stain using a clean, wet rag. If you have a wet/dry vacuum, use it to suck the moisture out of the spot. If not, let it dry completely before putting bedding back on.

MATTRESS-SAVING TIP

Consider getting a waterproof mattress cover for every bed in your house. This keeps your mattress as close to new as possible and protects it from any unwanted stains or smells. Plus, the mattress cover is washable!

How to Clean Curtains

Perhaps I should have titled this tutorial "You Should Maybe Think About Cleaning Your Curtains." This is a part of our home that is often overlooked and so, well, *dirty*.

How you wash your curtains will be determined by the fabric. Check whether they are machine washable (on the label or listed on the site from where you got them).

To Machine Wash Curtains

- Pretreat stains. Always sample stain remover on an inconspicuous spot to make sure it does not affect coloring.

- Machine wash on *gentle cycle* (sometimes called "delicate") with *cold water*.

- Dry them on low heat. I like to use dryer balls for items like this; they help speed the process and things dry more evenly.

- To prevent wrinkles, take the curtains out of dryer and hang them immediately. Alternatively, take out slightly damp curtains and hang them, lay them flat, or iron them.

To Hand Wash Curtains

- Fill a bathtub, large sink, or tote with lukewarm water. Add in a small amount of laundry detergent. If I was washing in my bathtub, for example, I'd use about 2 tablespoons (30 ml).

- Wash the curtains in the water by swirling them around and squeezing the fabric, making sure every part of the curtain is exposed thoroughly to soapy water.

- If the curtains are especially dirty, add in 1 cup (250 g) of borax before putting the curtains in the water. Let the curtains sit in the water for thirty minutes to an hour.

- Drain the dirty water and rinse the curtains. I like to rinse them under the faucet as best as I can, then fill up the tub or sink with clean water and rinse the curtains in that as well.

- Repeat until the water is clean with no dirt or soapy residue coming off the curtains.

- Wring out as much water as you can.

- Hang the curtains to dry on a sturdy drying line.

5.

The Bathroom

Ah, the bathroom. The place for laundry and toiletries and shampoo and water and too many strains of bacteria to count. It's wet. It's got the tendency to get smelly fast, and it takes so many steps to clean. Right now, I never know if I'm going to walk in and find rocks in the shower (toddler) and laundry on the floor (big kid). And there may be black soap residue on the white grout (husband . . . but seriously, who makes black soap and why do we have to buy it?!), or last night's brownie dish forgotten on the bath caddy (yours truly).

That means in my current stage of life, the bathrooms in my house take a fair amount of time out of my day to maintain order. Thankfully, with some well-thought-out habits and systems, I've made it so my time in the bathroom doing bathroom things coincides with putting things away and cleaning.

I notice right away if I haven't stayed on top of my habits and utilized my systems throughout the week. The bathroom gets messy and cluttered and so hard to actually clean. Yet with a few simple tweaks in your daily bathroom habits, you will notice a drastic difference in how much easier it is to maintain order in one of your hardest working rooms, as well as how much more straightforward it is to reset the space.

THE BATHROOM
Reset

STEP ONE: Put cleaning solution in the toilet bowl.

STEP TWO: Clear all the items out of the shower and bathtub. Toss anything that is empty in the trash. Rinse soap residue off the items and let them dry in the sink.

STEP THREE: Spray cleaner in the shower/tub.

STEP FOUR: Let the spray sit while you pick up the bathroom rug and throw the towels in the dirty laundry basket.

STEP FIVE: Scrub the shower/tub, then rinse.

STEP SIX: Take items out of the sink and place them back in the shower.

STEP SEVEN: Clean the toilet.

STEP EIGHT: Clear the bathroom counter and wipe it down with cleaner, including sinks and faucets.

STEP NINE: Wipe down the mirror.

STEP TEN: Wipe down the baseboards and walls as needed.

STEP ELEVEN: Empty the trash and replace the bag.

STEP TWELVE: Hang clean towels and washcloths.

STEP THIRTEEN: Vacuum or sweep the floors. This step is optional, but I find it useful to vacuum or sweep before mopping. When I don't, I notice that the mop doesn't pick up all the hair and lint, so I end up having to pick it up anyway.

STEP FOURTEEN: Mop the floors. Pour the dirty mop water in the toilet and let the bucket dry in the shower. Throw the dirty mop head in the wash.

STEP FIFTEEN: Replace the bathroom rug and put away the mop bucket when dry.

The Quick Bathroom
Reset

○ **Step One**
Clear the counters and
wipe them down.

○ **Step Two**
Scrub the toilet bowl.

○ **Step Three**
Spot clean the mirror.

○ **Step Four**
Vacuum and/or quick mop.

The Nightly Bathroom
Reset

○ **Step One**
Put everything on the
counter away.

○ **Step Two**
Hang up the towels and
put laundry in the basket.

○ **Step Three**
Do a quick wipe down of
the countertops.

The Bathroom Cleaning Arsenal

If there is any room in the house that needs its own arsenal of cleaning ammunition, it's the bathroom. I keep my arsenal in a cleaning caddy (a plastic tub with a handle to carry it) in the closet next to the bathroom. It is fully stocked with supplies to make it easy to grab and clean. These are the main components of a battle-ready bathroom arsenal (you may add in or use more as needed in your own space):

- All-purpose spray for counters and sinks (bonus if it also works on mirrors and bathtubs like my DIY recipe on page 45)
- Disinfectant spray or disinfectant wipes
- Roll of small trash bags
- Scrubber or cleaning brush
- Bathtub cleaner

- Toilet bowl cleaner: I keep mine tucked next to the toilet to clean the toilet any time it's needed (including outside of bathroom resets).
- Toilet brush: also tucked next to the toilet.
- Extendable shower scrubber

The Habits

Sometimes I feel silly when I incorporate a new habit and my life gets better. When I started putting away everything on my bathroom counter at night while I brushed my teeth, I felt like a dufus for not starting this little habit sooner. It didn't even take the full two minutes of brushing to put everything away, and yet for years I would go to bed with a cluttered bathroom counter and feel stressed first thing in the morning when I saw yesterday's mess.

Just like every other room in the house, micro habits make a macro impact. Unlike some other rooms in the house, however, your habitual prompts need a complete overhaul. The signals that reinforce bathroom habits are so engrained that they may not even be noticeable. A good example for me is my hairbrush. How many years has the prompt of finishing brushing my hair led me to the habit of setting the brush on my countertop and walking away?

When I recognize my patterns of behavior in this prompt-habit relationship, it makes it so much easier for me to break a cycle. Recognizing a prompt (e.g., finishing brushing or doing my hair) makes me aware of what habit I'd like to follow it with. When I finish brushing my hair, I open the bottom drawer and put the hairbrush in its designated spot. The reward is the pleasing visual of the brush neatly put away as well as the feeling of nicely brushed hair.

That is another aspect of helpful bathroom habits: They can become a part of your routine more easily once you recognize the importance of a signal (and satisfying result) in your daily rituals (the prompt and reward are already built in). All you need to change is the habit in the middle, which is mostly a quick fix. Your signal to brush your teeth is already built into your day, with the reward of fresh breath and clean teeth. The habit of putting your toothbrush away instead of on the counter takes a bit of extra brain effort in the beginning, but it takes less than five seconds more of your time each day.

If it helps, draw the habit loop on your bathroom mirror with dry erase marker. It'll wipe right off the mirror surface—don't worry! This will serve as a reminder to switch out the habit part of your normal loops to something that makes your daily life easier.

Consider incorporating these loop-disrupting bathroom habits into your everyday routine:

- **Clear the counter while you brush your teeth:** Put everything on your counter away in its designated spot while you brush your teeth morning and night. More on streamlining bathroom storage in the Systems section.

- **Post-facewash wipe down:** Keep a roll of paper towels or cleaning cloths under your sink. When you finish your nightly skin-care routine, wipe down the bathroom counter.

- **Hang up your towel:** If you are a chronic "wet towel on the bed" person, try changing your fresh-out-of-the-shower routine. Dry yourself off completely in the bathroom, and be a stickler for *not* taking the towel away from where it longs to remain—in the bathroom. If it helps, picture me walking into your room later in the day and exclaiming, "You left the wet towel on the bed again?! Now it's going to make the bed smell!" It worked for my husband. Of course, he got the real-life version of my towel on the bed wrath for the first several years of marriage, but I'm sure imaginary me could be just as scary.

- **Throw away things when they are empty:** Don't leave the shower without that empty shampoo bottle, and never put an empty toothpaste away in the drawer. The empty container in your hand is the reminder you need: Throw it away immediately because every day you are voting for the you who cares for yourself and your surroundings.

- **Give yourself the "ick":** The "ick" is a term Gen Z uses to describe the sudden onset of repulsion one feels in a relationship when a partner decides to wear toe shoes on a hike (or insert some other simple action that unwittingly creates a visceral response that can have no other label than "ick"). We can use this term to our advantage and use it introspectively. Pretend you are a stranger walking into your bathroom. What would give you the "ick"? Use that "ick" and reverse engineer a new way of being through "ick"-preventing habits.

SOME EXAMPLES OF "ICKS"

- **A less-than-sparkly toilet bowl:** When you open the toilet and get the "ick," it's time to clean it. You may not be able to clean it right at that moment, but you can set a reminder or an alarm for later that day.

- **The hair ball:** If you would never dream of clogging bathroom pipes with your hair and instead do the only thing reasonable and stick it to the shower wall like some sort of soggy modern art piece, it may be time to recognize this habit as "ick" inducing. I am humble and self-aware enough to realize that this is probably the only thing I do or have ever done that has given my husband the "ick." The solution is simple: Don't leave the shower empty-handed. When you reach for your towel, grab that hair ball and throw it away. If it helps, move the garbage can next to the shower for less resistance.

- **Stinky towels:** Hanging up towels to dry prevents a lot of stench, but it may be time to create a new helpful habit of washing your towels at least weekly. Consider picking one day a week as "towel day." This is the day you wash, dry, and put away your towels; bonus points for coordinating this with your bathroom reset time. I have more on how to deodorize towels in the laundry chapter (page 139) as well as fitting towels into your laundry routine (page 137).

- **Toothpaste splatter:** All it takes to solve this "ick" is a good rinse when you spit your toothpaste in the sink. Instead of spitting and walking away, make a new habit of rinsing *everything* down the drain before putting your toothbrush away and leaving the bathroom.

The Systems

By now you know my affinity for using clear bins to create smart storage systems. Streamlining bathroom storage can save so much time in your daily life. A well-organized bathroom also makes you feel more put together and calm during two of the most important parts of your day: the beginning and end.

Storage bins create a system that eliminates resistance, but this can mean different things for different people. Don't be afraid to think outside the box and experiment until your system serves you well and makes sense to you. I'll start with general tips for bathroom storage, then give specific ideas as a good jumping-off point in the Tutorials section.

Trash Talk

Not in the habit of throwing away used Q-tips, makeup wipes, or empty shampoo bottles? Maybe it's time to rehaul your bathroom trash system.

Identify the biggest resistance to throwing trash away. For me it was that the tiny bathroom trash can always felt full, and it was a pain in the behind to change. To eliminate resistance I could: Use a bigger garbage can. Empty the garbage can as part of a weekly routine. Or make it super easy to change out the trash bag.

I didn't have room for a bigger can, and I cannot remember to follow a weekly routine if it has too many steps, so that idea went out the window too. I ended up getting a multi-pack of small rolls of little trash can bags and keeping them in each bathroom. (I realized that running to a different room to get a bag was the step that always made me think "I'll do it later.") I also let myself consciously realize how much it bothered me to have a full trash can and used flossers on the counter. The system makes it easy to change out a trash bag and used my resistance in my favor (it feels worse to not change the trash).

Some systems to eliminate trash resistance in the bathroom:

- **Make it easy access:** Always keep the trash can where it is easy to use and easy to empty. Don't keep anything in front of it or block it.

- **Use bags:** Bags keep anything gunky, sticky, or smelly from getting in the can, and they make it easier to get rid of the trash.

- **Keep extra bags close by:** If you keep the bags in a cabinet near the trash or store them in the can directly underneath the current one, you'll have them at the ready.

- **Make sure it's functional:** If the trash can has a lid that is a pain to remove, get something easier to use. If it's an odd shape for where it is being stored and is a pain to get in and out, switch out the bin for a new one.

Flush the Fuss

You don't have to wait until you do a full reset to clean your toilet. Set up a system that removes resistance and makes it easy to clean. This will keep your bathroom feeling so much fresher. Here's what I do:

- **Keep the brush and bowl cleaner next to the toilet:** I keep mine right on the floor, tucked behind for easy access to just pour solution in and scrub when needed. My disinfectant wipes are close by as well, so I can wipe down anything unsavory quick.

- **Use toilet paper for dust:** It turns out, toilet paper works excellent to grab dust on the top of the toilet!

Towel Mildew Who?

Bacteria thrive in warm, dark, wet environments. Towels, washcloths, and bathroom rugs, or a pile of wet towels on your floor are all perfect breeding grounds for stench-causing bacteria. Those same bacteria can cause acne when you use the towels! Needless to say, your bathroom will be a lot more pleasant when you have systems to let towels dry between uses. (For how to wash and eliminate odors in bathroom linens, flip to page 139.)

Something as simple as switching out your towel bar for hooks can be revolutionary when it comes to the bathroom towel dilemma. Currently my master bathroom is remodeled, but the bathroom that kids and guests use is not. In my master bath we installed hooks, both for hand towels and bath towels. There are never towels on my floor—not even when my kids use my bathroom.

The other bathroom is a completely different story. The hand towel hook by the sink "fell off" the wall after we moved in, and all the towels end up on the floor or hung haphazardly on the towel bar by the shower. I can't wait to tackle this bathroom in the remodel and switch out those dumb towel bars. I know the bathroom will function better instantly.

If the thought of drywall anchors and drills scares you, adding in towel hooks can be as easy as getting a package of removable wall hooks and adding them in the bathroom. They have a sticky backing and can be removed without causing damage to the wall, and they even make ones that look like a real metal hook you'd screw into the wall! Just be sure to get ones that are sturdy enough to hold your towels: Pay attention to the weight recommendations. The package will say how much the hook can hold.

Hooks can also be used for robes, washcloths, hair towels, dry brushes, loofas, or anything else you find hanging out on the bathroom counter (or floor) that you want easy access to while keeping it out of the way.

The Backup Supply System

Backup toilet paper and hygiene items can take up a lot of space in the bathroom. During our master bathroom remodel, we all used one bathroom (with *no* storage) and one tiny linen closet that was stuffed to the brim. *Something* was always falling off the shelves.

Our hygiene suffered. Our mental health suffered. And our ability to find things when we needed them suffered. It was a real reminder of the importance of systems, and how much easier a functional home makes day-to-day life.

Creating a backup system that eliminates resistance and creates easy access to what you need is so important:

- **Keep toilet paper by the toilet:** If someone in your household "forgets" to replace the roll, you can at least reach it when you need it most. I like keeping a stack of rolls in the cabinet next to or above the toilet, with my backup stash in the linen closet. When I use the last roll or notice it getting low in the bathroom, I'll take two to three rolls from the linen closet and stock the bathroom again.

- **Split the storage into zones:** Keep extra toilet paper within reach of the toilet. The same goes with feminine hygiene products. Washcloths and facewash make sense under the sink, and use top drawers for the items you need for your daily routine. Backup items you don't need every day can go wherever you have space to store them, placed behind more in-demand items.

- **Get creative with solutions:** Keep a cute little box with a lid on top of the toilet tank with TP and feminine hygiene products. If you have a little wiggle room space- and budget-wise, purchase a cabinet that goes above the toilet but has legs that stretch to the ground so you don't have to install it on the wall. Switching out your mirror for a medicine cabinet mirror can also add a lot of storage space.

The Cute or Clutter System

I have a bathtub caddy that takes pride of place on my soaker tub. As soon as we finished the remodel, I whipped that bad boy out, set it on the tub, and added a cute little candle and fancy washcloth to "style" it. Lovely, yes, but there was no room for my brownie on the caddy when all was said and done. Decide if your décor is serving you or adding clutter to your day. The candle was cute, but not cute enough to not be clutter.

Take a good look at your bathroom items and decide if they're cute or clutter.

Cute
Something cute serves a purpose: whether it is cute and adds to the whole ambiance, or whether it is pretty and serves a purpose for you too. Some examples include:

- A candle that you light every day that stays in the same spot.

- A jewelry box that you keep on the counter and use most days.

- Pretty glass jars you keep on the counter that hold cotton balls and Q-tips you use in your daily routine.

- An antiqued brass magnifying mirror on the counter you use every day to look for stray hairs to tweeze. Thankfully you've never had any.

Clutter
Clutter sometimes may be cute, but it gets in the way and doesn't serve a purpose. Some examples include:

- A pretty candle on your bathtub caddy you never light and have to move every night to make room for your brownie (or cookie dough).

- A gorgeous tray, like the one you saw on Pinterest, to hold your bathroom supplies—but ends up collecting water under it every time you use it. It is constantly in need of a wipe down, and it's a pain to move to clean your countertops.

- A glass vase that you hate cleaning around. And it always seems to be in the way and serves no real function.

- Eliminate clutter. Remember: Being visually appealing is a purpose for an item. I'm not telling you to get rid of all your décor. Just truthfully weigh the benefits of each item, and make sure it deserves to be where it is. It has to be serving you, not the other way around.

The Tutorials

A Step-by-Step Guide to Bathroom Organization

STEP ONE: Grab a garbage bin.

STEP TWO: Find easy storage solutions that fit in your drawers or cupboards.

STEP THREE: Go through one drawer or shelf at a time.

- **Remove EVERYTHING:** Throw away anything you have not used in the past three months, anything you don't like, or anything expired.

- **Sort the remaining item:** Use categories that make sense for your life. See page 103 for ideas to categorize your bathroom storage.

- **Wipe down each drawer or shelf:** Vacuum first if needed. Then place the storage bins in the clean drawers or cupboard. Put every item in a category in one bin (e.g., hair products, face wash, dental items).

- **Give everything a place:** If things are loose, instead of in a bin or organizer, the clutter easily gets out of hand. If it helps, label the bins using a label maker or simply a Sharpie (which will wipe off plastic with acetone on a cotton pad). Defining the space and its uses creates a system that you will actually adhere to.

STEP FOUR: Declutter your counter.

- **Relocate rarely used items when you can:** Add the items you keep on your counter (but add clutter) to the categories you made in drawers or cupboards.

STORAGE SOLUTION IDEAS

- Grab plastic storage bins at the dollar store. (They even have fun colors!) Make sure to measure your drawers or cupboards before you purchase.

- Repurpose old boxes or baskets into storage solutions. I use rectangular or square pieces that don't have any curve or change in width so they fit together nicely without wasting space.

- **Do you really need it out all the time?** Consider keeping your bathroom counter completely cleared off except for soap.

STEP FIVE: Minimize other clutter.

- Keep one towel per person hung up: I recently got color-coded towels for my husband and I so we each have our own and know whose is whose.

- Get a basket with a lid for dirty clothes: This keeps everything in one place, and visually it won't look or feel like clutter.

- Consider function above all else: If you have a pretty bathroom rug that doesn't stay put and is always in the way, consider adding a sticky backing to it or getting something more functional. Be ruthless! This room is meant to serve *you*.

Categorizing Your Bathroom Storage

- **By purpose:** "Hair," "Nails," "Face Wash," etc.

- **By routine:** I recently reorganized my bathroom drawer by routine and LOVE it. I grouped all of my morning routine products together, then evening, then makeup, etc. It has been so much easier to find everything and put it back in the right spot, and I have been better about doing my skin-care routines ever since.

- **By brand:** If you have sets of products, you may want to group things by brand.

- **By usage:** You may find that categorizing items based on how much you use them works best for you. For example, one basket under the sink may contain your dryer, heat protectant spray, and favorite brush, while the rest of your hair stuff is in a different basket or bin tucked away behind it.

THE GERMAPHOBE'S GUIDE TO TOILET CLEANING

I have toilet cleaning down to a science. I attribute this to the fact that in the dental hygiene program I graduated from in college, we spent a significant amount of time learning how to sanitize things and eliminate cross contamination with anything "dirty." Our first clinical exam was on how to wash hands like a surgeon and was one of the most nerve-racking moments of my life. I may not use the degree I paid an arm and a leg (and my sanity) for anymore, but I still know my way around destroying germs.

Start with the Supplies

- A disinfecting toilet bowl cleaner. I am sensitive to fragrance, so I use one that doesn't feel like my nose hairs are burning off while I'm cleaning.

- A more-bang-for-your-buck toilet brush. Spend a few extra dollars and get a toilet bowl brush that is engineered to let the brush drip dry without sitting in dirty water (and can be cleaned) and you will eliminate a lot of unnecessary smell.

- Disposable disinfectant wipes.

- Cleaning gloves only for cleaning the toilet. Store these in a zip-top bag after they dry out to avoid contaminating anything else.

The Steps

- Put on the gloves.

- Pour the toilet solution in the bowl and let it sit while you wipe down the exterior.

- Using disposable wipes, wipe down the toilet: Start with the handle and top of the tank. Move to the lid, then the seat, then the rest of the toilet. Use however many wipes you'd like. Then use disinfecting wipes to clean the floor around the toilet and the toilet base.

- Scrub the toilet with the toilet brush, then rest the toilet brush between the bowl and seat to dry with the brush facing in toward the bowl.

- Remove the gloves and let them dry. I store mine in a plastic bag in a bathroom cupboard.

- Wash hands with soap and water.

How to Clean Grout

I thought I was soooooo clever choosing white grout to go with my white tile in my bathroom. Visually, it's stunning. Maintaining it is a nightmare. My favorite way to clean grout is a household staple you may be able to guess (because by now we are BFFs): baking soda.

My shower floor has a lot of little tiles all held together with *a lot* of white grout. It's so much to clean around! I found that sprinkling baking soda on the floor, spraying with my vinegar-based All-Purpose Spray (page 45), then letting it sit for a few minutes before scrubbing with a brush lifts so much stain!

To save your back or if you have mobility issues, get a scrub brush or pad on an extension pole. It makes cleaning the shower floors and walls so much easier.

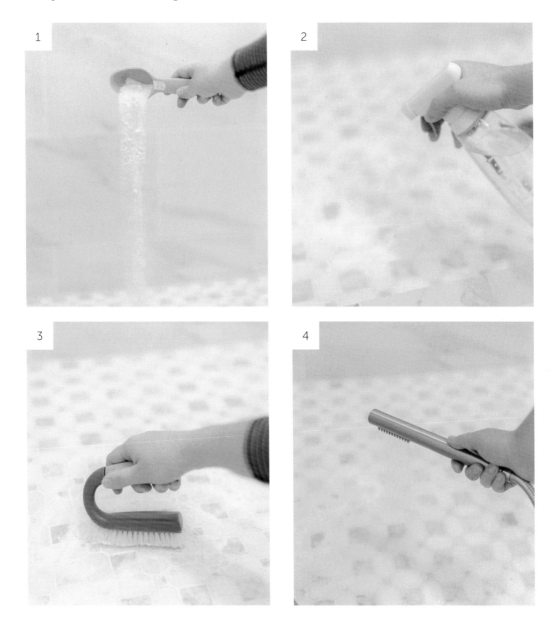

Streak-Free Glass

I accidentally figured out the most magical way to clean glass. When I was coming out of a year-long chronic illness rut where I was not able to function at all, I was bound and determined to look into other ways that I could support my health (and hopefully not lose another entire year of mine and my family's lives). I decided to start choosing healthier options for cleaning products in my home, and was specifically looking for stainless steel cleaners that didn't give me an instant headache and had natural ingredients.

I stumbled upon these cleaning cloths called NanoTowels that claimed to work with "just water." Turns out, they really do work with just water—and on glass too! Over the years I couldn't tell you how many different cleaning products I have bought for windows and mirrors. Everything left streaks. And if it did a halfway decent job, it was so full of chemicals that I felt like I was going to pass out from inhaling the fumes.

Now, honest to goodness, I use water and a NanoTowel. I have a whole closet stash and use them for everything. I get half the towel wet and wipe down the mirror or shower door, then dry with the other side. Streak free and clean, instantly! If there is a lot of hard water stain on the shower door I will use my All-Purpose Spray and then the NanoTowel.

How to Clean Drains

Shower and sink drains are another sneaky place that can create foul odors in your bathroom. Drains are also one of those aspects of you home that you take for granted until they aren't functioning—then it feels like a disaster. Here are the best ways my husband and I have figured out (with the help of plumbers) to keep drains clean in the bathroom:

- **Be proactive with an enzyme treatment:** This was a great tip from our plumber. He recommended pouring an enzyme solution down our bathroom drains periodically. This type of cleaner biologically breaks down the "stuff" that builds up in pipes over time. It'll help keep your plumbing working smoothly and eliminate any odors.

- **Be careful what you put down the drain:** For example, if you add in oil-pulling to your oral routine, don't ever spit down the sink. Coconut oil will solidify and build up in your pipes.

- **Have a hair plan:** Trust me, you don't want to have to dig a hair clog out of a drain. Don't rinse your hair down the drain if you can help it. There are drain inserts available to collect hair.

- **Keep a drain snake on hand:** Find these online or at a hardware store. They are easy to use and can remove clogs.

- **When in doubt, call a professional!**

6.

Entry Spaces

I once read a lovely book about French
homemaking, and the author talked about how
the French design their entrance as a literal
welcome into their home from the world outside
and include little items that tell the guest a bit
of the story of the homeowners. When looking
around my entryway with this perspective,
I realized that a guest walking in might feel
confusion at seeing the modest size of the house
compared to the seemingly endless number
of people living there (based on the amount
of clothes and shoes strewn about). Then they
would promptly trip over the bunched-up rug.

Whether you want to romanticize the design of the entrance to your home or not, you deserve to have a welcoming space that functions well. It doesn't need to be fancy or complicated, but it does have to do its job.

So go ahead, take a moment to ponder how you feel when you enter your home.

Now think about how you *want* it to feel. This can be harder, but I'll give you my example: I want it to feel welcoming and homey, like there is a lovely grandmother ushering me in. She is warm and smells nice, takes my coat and keys to hang them up, and helps me shrug out of my jacket to put it in its designated spot. She probably gives me a hug and calls me "dear."

Perhaps you want your entrance to function similarly but with a different vibe. Perhaps it is all about precise organization as if there is a butler nearby helping keep everything right where you need it, whether you are fighting crime by day or schmoozing at galas by night.

Either way, we are going to establish the systems and habits to have an entryway that's ready to greet us well.

THE ENTRYWAY

Reset

STEP ONE: Gather the coats and clothes. Hang the coats currently in use. Set any extra coats or clothes not in use next to the entrance to the space to put away at the end of the reset. For example, rain jackets that take up valuable hanging space when it's not in a rainy season, or winter coats hanging in the entry during summer. Hats, scarves, or any other outerwear kept in the entryway should be put away.

STEP TWO: Tidy the shoes currently in use or put them away in the entryway. Set any shoes not in season or not being used next to the entrance.

STEP THREE: Hang the keys in a designated area.

STEP FOUR: Sort and take care of the mail. Trash gets tossed in the bin, and the rest of the mail gets put in a designated spot.

STEP FIVE: Put miscellaneous items away where they belong. If they don't belong in the entryway, set them by the entrance.

STEP SIX: Dust top to bottom.

STEP SEVEN: Wipe down the windows, doors, walls, and baseboards as needed. Wipe down the door handles and light switches with a disinfecting wipe, especially during cold and flu season.

STEP EIGHT: Tidy and straighten anything else on the floor (e.g., furniture, etc.), and remove the rug. Shake the rug off outside.

STEP NINE: Sweep/vacuum and mop.

STEP TEN: Put away the items left by the entrance where they belong.

STEP ELEVEN: Replace the rug.

The Quick Entryway

○ **Step One**
Hang the coats.

○ **Step Two**
Tidy the shoes.

○ **Step Three**
Vacuum and straighten the rug.

The Habits

My husband was a chronic lock-keys-in-the-car guy when I met him (and let's be real, for the first several years of marriage as well). Thanks to newer cars with key fobs, he hasn't locked us out of the car for a long time, but lately we have been losing keys a lot again. The reason? Our habits are out of whack and our entering-the-home systems are obliterated.

Initially I thought writing this book while we destroyed and rebuilt our home was entirely foolish and more than a little hypocritical. The entrance to my home currently has no floor, and there are holes in the drywall big enough to stick your head through. There's not even a light fixture; we've been using a battery-powered shop light that somehow is never charged.

But as I write, I realize the timing seems to be a (backhanded) blessing: Not for my stress levels, but for the fact that I am reworking systems and habits from scratch again. And also because I must lean on them while surrounded by utter chaos and more resistance to a peaceful home than I've ever felt before in my life.

I'm proving to myself that a small tweak in habits and systems can create calm in chaos. Someday I'll have my Mrs. Pots greeting when I walk into my home, but for now I'll settle for a reluctant nail in the unfinished drywall by the door to hang keys. These are the bare bones habits that will set the foundation for a welcoming entryway:

Hang Up Your Keys, Dang It!

The entryway welcomes you into your home, and it's your last-ditch effort to leave in a calm state as well. I hate leaving my home like a tornado: trying to scoop up anything close by that may be of use in a whirl of chaos, and leaving disaster in my wake as I head out the door. When we have an entrance that is set up to function well and the habits to keep it that way, leaving the house is soooo much less stressful. Starting with keys. Make the habit of hanging up your keys as soon as you walk through the door.

I have some specific and tangible ideas for key storage options in the Systems section of this chapter, but right now we will work on how to cement this habit into your routine.

- **Always put your keys where they belong:** Do this as soon as you walk in the door. If you need to, put a sticky note on your door to remind yourself.

- **Cement the habit:** Do this every time, even if it's clunky, until the habit sticks.

- **Reward:** Acknowledge for a moment how nice it is to leave the house without frantically trying to find your keys.

Shoes in Their Spot

Get into the practice of leaving your shoes in the same spot, whether that is by the entrance or put away. If you enter the house most often through your garage, don't miss out on using that space! Use a rug and shoe rack and make it a nice little spot to take your shoes off before you enter the home.

If you have kids, keeping up with this habit yourself will help instill the same in them. My toddler likes his cowboy boots and wants to wear them in the house. With the repetition every single day of taking off his boots on the step in our garage and setting them on the rack, he is starting to get into the routine more and will sit down on the step by himself waiting for help with his shoes (sometimes).

Coat Hung Up and Backpacks off the Floor

Coats, backpacks, purses, and bags all should be hung up. They will be ready to go when you need them and out of the way when you are using the space.

Sort Your Mail

As I'm writing this section I'm realizing I need to go dig a medical bill out of the car because I need to pay it before I get late fees. My mail habits are still all messed up, because at the moment our home entrance (and every other space) is messed up. The only consistent and beneficial mail habit I currently have is tossing junk mail in the outside garbage instead of bringing it inside. The rest is a free-for-all.

If you've been an adult for any number of years, you know mail is important. It may even give you anxiety (like that medical bill I thought insurance was going to cover). Our habits can take care of that postal tension in our daily life if we get creative with it:

- **Have a designated mail spot:** Find a space that is a convenient drop zone when you enter the house. You want it to be easy to keep organized. (We'll cover specifics in the Systems section.)

- **Toss the junk immediately:** This step is a huge help when it comes to keeping your mail system from getting out of hand. Any obvious "junk" goes straight in the trash or recycling without being set down with the rest of your mail.

- **Keep your coupons where you can find them:** If you use coupons, put them in an envelope in your purse or as a separate section in your mail spot.

- **Sort the rest:** Bills, letters, magazines, etc. each go in their own designated area.

- **Pick a day:** Take care of your mail on a set day very week. This day is for paying bills, tossing old magazines, and filing away anything you keep.

The Systems

The main focus of entrance habits is to keep everything out of the way *and* easily accessible. That can make for some tension and resistance in the space, which is why our systems must be extra smart and hardworking. For example, we've been losing keys because we don't have a place to put the keys. There is no place for our habits to rest, so they bounce around in perpetual chaos. Our systems are what bring the spirit of the entryway alive (whether that be Mrs. Pots or Gollum).

Find Your Frequent Offender

What aspect of your entry space is the most cumbersome? Is it the inability to get out the door without tripping over shoes? Always-missing-keys syndrome? School backpack chaos? Figure out what isn't working for you, then build systems that make it possible for the habits to stick. Here are some system ideas that match up directly with the habits in the last section.

Chronic Missing Key Syndrome

The easiest, most effective system I have found to keep track of keys is a simple hook right inside the door. There are endless options to fit your décor, or simply hang them on a nail or removable hook. If you have a table in your entryway, a basket, box, or drawer is another easy option. Just throw your keys in when you get home. However, remember that sometimes opening a drawer or pulling off a lid can act as resistance and keep you from sticking to your habit. The easier, the better.

Mismatched Shoe Mountain

We tend to take shoes off in the garage, so we set up some shelving right outside the door and often take our shoes off before entering the house. We have tried shoe sorters and shelves, but I notice the shoes never made it in the sorters. One of the

easiest ways we kept shoes tidy at our last house was baskets; they slid under the bench in our entryway and my big kid could toss her shoes in and get them out.

Coats Taking Over the World

I firmly believe any storage system that does not involve an easy-to-hang-on hook creates too much resistance. My favorite system for coat and backpack storage is adding peg hooks to the wall. I love the look of them, and ain't nothin' fallin' off those hooks. You can also hang these hooks farther down the wall to hold boots.

Mail Malady

Mail can be one of those aspects of running a household that can become such a headache if you don't have a system that works for you. Bills can get lost, outgoing mail misplaced, and birthday invitations found months after the party date. Having a hardworking mail system in place can make life run so much more smoothly.

- **Mini post office:** In case you didn't notice, I never grew out of the overactive-imagination stage in childhood. If you're weird like me, have fun making a little post office in your house complete with a rubber return label and fun stamps. If you aren't, just keep your stamps and envelopes close to where you sort your mail. This takes away the resistance to your taking-care-of-business day when you pay bills.

- **Junk management:** Consider keeping a garbage or recycling bin close by to reinforce your habit of tossing junk mail immediately.

- **Mail sorter:** To save space, get a sorter with multiple slots that hangs on the wall; sort as you put your mail away every day. If you have ample space in your home entrance, there are tabletop or drawer options as well. Another favorite of mine is an expanding or accordion file folder. This is what I use to sort the current years' documents, and it is handy to keep by the mail sorter to file away paid bills. It can also double as your mail sorter and save a step!

- **Grocery obstacle course:** Have you seen the videos of people who put a "Costco door" in their pantry? It's a mini door that opens from the garage into their super fancy pantry, so they can stuff all their groceries directly through the mini door and bypass carrying them around. We can't all have "Costco doors," or even pantries for that matter, but we do all have to eat.

How easy is it for you to make your way into your home and to the kitchen? How about with all the bags of groceries cutting into your wrists so you only have to make one trip? When we nail our habits and systems for the entryway, anything we have to tote through should be a breeze.

One system that may help with this weekly obstacle is keeping a clear surface to temporarily set things down. Whether that's a bench, shelf, or table, keeping space open to set groceries down while you hang your keys will make life easier.

Not-So-Welcome Guests

Now that we've Mrs. Pots-ed our entryways to the best of our abilities, we get to step in and take part in the welcoming when guests come. Having a system in place to hang a guests' coat and scarf will make them feel welcome and make you feel put together.

If you use a different entrance than your guests, it is worthwhile to think through a system for when you host:

- Keep space in the coat closet and extra hangers.
- Utilize hooks or a coat rack for easy storage and access.
- Have open space for guests to set things down.
- Consider how guests would need or like to use furniture (e.g., a bench to sit and tie shoes).

Thinking Outside the "Shoe" Box

Every home entrance is soooo different in terms of space and layout. And everyone tends to wear shoes differently (e.g., wear in the house or not, same pair most days or switch out every day, etc.). Don't be afraid to think outside the box, or try some of these ideas:

- **Shoe basket:** Have a basket or bin close to the door for everyone to toss their shoes in. I like having metal bins with removable linen liners that I can remove, shake out, and wash if needed.

- **Bench with hidden storage:** I like to have a bench in my entryway for people to sit on when they take their shoes off, mostly to make up for being a total stickler for making people take their shoes off in my house. Some benches open up with hidden storage or built-in bins underneath. Make your entryway furniture work hard for its spot!

- **Over-the-door shoe sorter:** If you have a closet in your entryway, try adding a small shelf at the bottom or hang a shoe sorter over the inside of the closet door. Just make absolutely sure you will use it!

- **Storage cabinet:** There are so many smart options for entryway storage! Get or build lockers with shoe storage. Get cabinets that look pretty and save space that are designed specifically for shoes. Do some digging online to find something that will work for your space, or head to the thrift store and pick up a used cabinet or console table. Try putting shoe bins in the bottom and use the rest for outerwear storage.

- **No Shoe policy:** It may work best for you or your family to have a "No Shoes in the Entryway" policy. You may consider this if you have a tight space that is the only (or most frequent) way in and out of the house. This will mean some serious habit-building along with a good shoe storage system in a bedroom or closet.

The Tutorials

Spot Cleaning a Rug

Sometimes the ol' "beat the rug on the front porch" tactic just doesn't cut it. If your entryway rug is looking a little worse for wear, spot clean it or do the full-meal-deal rug clean. Disclaimer: You'll need some time and space. Also, if you have an antique, Persian, or expensive rug, hire a professional!

Spot clean a rug the same as you would carpet. I use a dab of castile soap and a wet, clean rag and dab at the spot. I let it sit for a few minutes, then rinse with a clean, wet (with only water) rag, and repeat until the stain lifts. Or use a portable carpet spot cleaner as you would for upholstery or carpet.

For the full meal deal, make sure you have a couple of hours to dedicate to the process. You'll also want good weather, a hose, and a spot to dry the rug:

STEP ONE: Shake off any dust or debris from the rug.

STEP TWO: Clean off the area where you will clean the rug. I like to do this on the (clean) concrete driveway at a bit of a decline so the water can run off. Learn from my mistakes and do not do this on the lawn. Once the area is prepped, lay the rug flat.

STEP THREE: Spray the rug with a hose on a "jet" setting that sprays hard in a direct line, and rinse off the rug.

STEP FOUR: Dilute a small amount of dish soap in a bucket of warm water (if the rug is wool, use cold water). Use a soft-bristled scrub brush to work the soap into the rug, spending extra time on stains.

STEP FIVE: Use the hose to rinse the rug thoroughly. If needed, scrub any lingering stains.

STEP SIX: Remove the excess water. The first time I did this I tried to lift up the rug and shake off and let the excess water drip off, and instead I looked like I was losing a battle to some two-dimensional sea monster. Save your neighbors a show and use a wet/dry vac or squeegee to remove as much water as you can.

STEP SEVEN: Let the rug dry completely. This is where the patience and time come in. In my experience rugs take a long time to dry. I like to hang mine over the deck railing in the sun. But don't forget about it; the sun can fade things quickly. If you leave a wet rug laying flat on the concrete, it will trap moisture under it and will not dry. If you leave a wet rug to dry in the hot sun on grass, it will leave a large dead spot underneath it and your husband will say "PLEASE don't do stuff like this in the grass anymore, Karissa."

P.S. There are now washable rugs available that you can throw in the washing machine! Even better.

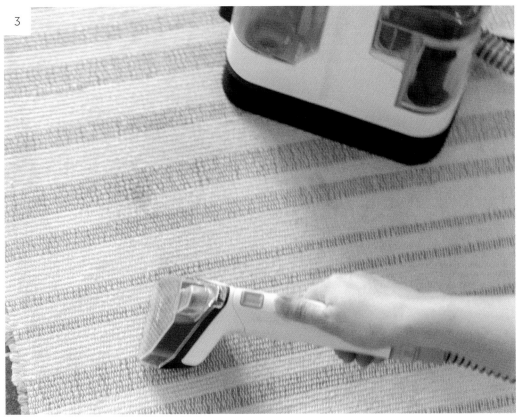

How to Clean Your Walls

The entry spaces in our homes can really take a beating. I notice scuff marks from kicked-off shoes and mystery substances on the walls. (Is that applesauce or snot?)

- **Scuff-mark spot cleaning:** I swear by melamine sponges for scuff marks on walls, doors, and trim. Be sure to test a spot, and make sure your paint can hold up to scrubbing.

- **Clean the whole wall:** Use warm water with a dash of dish soap in a mop bucket, then simply mop the walls. Make sure the mop is damp, not soaking. Go over the walls with just water (again, damp, not soaking) to ensure there is no soap residue left. Alternatively, use this same method with a damp cloth.

7.

The Laundry Room

I would love to be the person who tells you that all it takes is a change of perspective and you will suddenly see laundry as the blessing it is. Dear reader, I'm not that person. No amount of visualization or gratitude journaling has changed the fact that an ever-growing pile of laundry is the bane of my existence at worst and a pestering nuisance on the best day.

Laundry has always been an aspect of running my home that I find challenging. My first apartment had a mold problem, and the washer and dryer always made all our clothes smell mildewy. Our first home had a great setup for laundry, but as a first-time mom who was battling chronic illness, there were always piles of dirty clothes and never the time, health, or willpower to keep up on it. We then moved into a house that had a laundry room in the basement with the bedrooms upstairs. I wasn't battling with chronic illness in the same severe way, but at times I still felt too dizzy to do anything but crawl up and down the stairs. It was in that home that I realized that I needed to find a system that would make keeping up on laundry doable.

In our current home, I can still remember a time shortly after we moved in: A behemoth of a microwave was sitting in the middle of the floor of the laundry room as we remodeled. (If you could even call it a floor at the time; we had ripped out the old floor and had yet to replace it.) There was not a countertop or shelf to hold laundry supplies, and I had to hold my half-broken washing machine lid just right to get it to latch and start.

Despite having those obstacles for months as we focused on the primary rooms and let the laundry room sit, we never fell that far behind. When our washer and dryer were being replaced, finally, my mom very generously offered to come pick up my laundry and do it for me. (Best gift ever!) As she picked up the laundry to bring it to her house and do it, she said, "You've got to have more than that!" I was so proud of myself. What felt like a lot of laundry I was behind on was so much less than what it would have been years prior, when I didn't have habits in place keeping me on track.

THE LAUNDRY ROOM

Reset

STEP ONE: Put washing machine cleaner in the empty washing machine and run it on hot. This is not necessary every time you reset your laundry room; I do this about once a month.

STEP TWO: Check your stock of detergent, softener, and laundry supplies. Refill as needed.

STEP THREE: Empty the lint trap in the dryer and vacuum out any excess.

STEP FOUR: Wipe down the dryer.

STEP FIVE: Wipe down the countertops, shelves, and cabinets as needed.

STEP SIX: Wipe down the walls, windows, and baseboards as needed.

STEP SEVEN: When the washer finishes the self-clean cycle, wipe down the inside of the washing machine. Make sure to wipe down every nook and cranny. Washing machines are notorious for having hidden parts that grow mold and collect gunk. Take out the detergent dispenser and clean it. If needed, soak it in hot water and vinegar to remove buildup.

STEP EIGHT: Empty the trash and replace the bag.

STEP NINE: Vacuum/sweep and mop the floors. Start at the point farthest from the door and work your way toward the door.

The Quick Laundry Room

Reset

◯ **Step One**
Clean up any clothes and store them in a hamper or toss them in the washing machine.

◯ **Step Two**
Tidy surfaces. Put away detergent or any other objects that are out of place.

◯ **Step Three**
Sweep or vacuum the floor.

The Habits

You know the age-old rhyme "A load a day keeps the laundry scaries away"? Yeah, me either. But figuring out your laundry habits once and for all may just push you to write a sonnet or some folklore rhyme to pass down to the generations after you. A lean, mean laundry routine will make your days and weeks go so much smoother, and it is worth taking the time to iron it out.

A Load a Day

Let me be the first to say, sometimes this isn't feasible. But whether you struggle with physical limitations like I do, have limited access to a washing machine, or just plain don't have the time, utilize the spirit of this habit. To keep on top of laundry, don't let it build up.

For me, with my current family size, that looks like doing at least one load of laundry six days a week. I have a sample laundry schedule printout on page 169. Doing a load of laundry means washing it, drying it, folding it, and putting it away. No mismatched socks left behind! Easier said than done, right? Well, here are some practical tips to get in the groove of incorporating laundry into your (daily) routine:

If You Work from Home
Find a time to start laundry every day: Try after you get dressed in the morning, when you change out of your workout clothes, after you shower, or when you lay the kids down for a nap. Pick a time when it seems like a natural extension of your routine to start a load.

If You Work outside the Home
Find a time to squeeze in a load of laundry: Put clothes and detergent in the washer before bed, then press the button to start a load before you leave for work in the morning. Or maybe it makes more sense to begin a load as you walk in the door from work.

If You Have Kids
Get your kids in the habit of helping: Set a reminder or use a chart to pick a day for that child's laundry to be done. Start at any age: My big kid is starting to learn how to do her own laundry, and I'm working on my toddler starting to help throw things in the wash (while keeping him from climbing in).

Cement the Habit

Find a laundry detergent with a scent you love, or have a morning cup of coffee ready to enjoy after you start a load. Get creative with this part of your routine!

Remembering to Switch the Laundry

This is an important habit to get in place. I am the queen of forgetting to switch the laundry, and this is probably my biggest obstacle to completing a load of laundry every day.

If You Work from Home

Find a consistent reminder: Lunchtime could be a great time to check on the laundry. When you get up from eating, head to the laundry room and toss everything in the dryer. If you struggle to remember to stop what you are doing and head to the laundry room to switch as soon as the load is done, try setting an alarm on your phone or turning the audio level up loud enough on your washer to hear it when it is done. The key is having a consistent prompt to associate with "time to switch the laundry," so it's great to get creative with it!

If You Work outside the Home

Switch it when you walk in the door: If the laundry is clean and waiting in the washing machine when you get home, take care of it first thing when you get home. If you begin the load when you get home, try switching it after dinner or right before putting the kids to bed.

If You Have Kids

Let switching the laundry be a daily chore for them! This can be a simple, fun (depending on the kid), and very "responsible" part of their day. Both of my kids like to help switch the laundry. Keep it at a consistent time in your day (e.g., after homework is done and before dinner).

Incorporate a Reward

You can use your sense of smell for this habit as well—like tossing a dryer ball scented with drops of your favorite essential oil in the load when you switch it, or adding a yummy smelling dryer sheet. A reward also can be as simple as a pat on the back or a "Good job, me!"

Folding the Laundry

Habit stacking is a great way to make yourself really stick with the dreaded task of folding and putting away the laundry. Take a habit that you enjoy and stack folding laundry on top of it. I felt like my eyes were opened to a whole new world when my aunt mentioned watching TV while she folded and put away laundry. As dumb as it sounds, I had never once considered doing something enjoyable when folding and putting away laundry. Now, I make sure to listen to something, watch something, or sip something I enjoy while folding and putting away laundry. That one small shift made a huge difference in this habit for me.

If You Work from Home
Pick a time in your day or night when you consistently have a moment to focus on this one task: If your brain likes to respond right away to the dryer being done, do it then. Otherwise, spend time folding during your nightly comfort show or the twenty-minute brainless break you need every afternoon. Find something that consistently works for you.

If You Work outside the Home
Stacking this habit: Pairing laundry with something enjoyable can be even more beneficial if your hours to keep up on housework are crammed into a smaller amount of time. Using something like your nightly show or podcast to watch or listen to while you fold laundry can make that time, dare I say, pleasant.

If You Have Kids
Teach them to fold—or at the very least put their laundry away! Their prompt to join in and help is seeing you begin this process, or when you finish and announce it's time to put laundry away. We will talk about more ways to make this work with kids in our Systems section.

Incorporate a Reward
I am a big fan of dessert rewards for getting through the laundry (or day). If a sweet treat is not up your alley, use habit stacking to add in your reward.

If you are reading this with a burning desire to tell me "Yeah right Karissa, there's no possible way I can fit in a load of laundry every day," I understand completely. Let's talk habits that will help keep you on top of laundry:

- **Consistency is key:** However it fits in your life, find consistency. Whether it's Wednesdays and Fridays or an all-out laundry marathon every Saturday, figure out a way to count on yourself to get the laundry done consistently every week. Whether this means penciling it on your calendar or using the full laundry basket as your signal to start washing, make consistency your friend.

- **Make the time:** If you do several loads of laundry in a batch, have a plan for how to make the time to actually complete the laundry. This may be a two-day process: washing and drying one day and folding the next, or a big pile of clean clothes waiting to fold and put away at the end of the day. The important part of laundry isn't in the

logistics, but in finding habits that work toward making your life easier (and clean clothes available whenever you need them).

- **Make it a ritual:** There's no need to get religious about your laundry habits, but having some sort of ritual (an established rhythm and routine) can help you stay on top of things. Find your signal to do laundry, and make the rest a habit your body does on its own.

Dirty Laundry in the Basket

I have always despised stepping around piles of dirty clothes on the floor, yet for most of my life I had a brain block when it came to putting my dirty clothes in the laundry basket. It doesn't make a whole lot of sense to live in your home in a way that doesn't bring you peace, and yet it is so easy to have habits that do just that. I couldn't tell you when I began putting my clothes in the dirty laundry basket instead of the floor, then going even further and turning them right-side out before putting them in the laundry basket, but it has made a huge difference in how much I enjoy my bedroom and bathroom.

This prompt is so, so simple, but the habit itself may be a steep, uphill battle

PUT AWAY YOUR LAUNDRY BASKET

When you finish your load of laundry, put away the basket where it belongs. Do not allow yourself to leave a laundry basket out. If I do this in my house, it seems like an open invitation to put stuff in it. Random dirty clothes (or were they clean?!), toy trucks, things to put away, or my toddler's half-eaten cracker will begin to fill up a laundry basket in the middle of the floor.

Put the laundry basket away when you put the laundry away. Empty that thing completely. Trust me, you will not put those washcloths you left in there away tomorrow. Someone's going to sneak in and dump a bunch of dirty clothes on the clean washcloths and pretty soon a week will have passed and you can't remember what was at one point clean.

We'll chat more about systems for laundry basket storage in the next section, because I know that they can be difficult to store. For now, remember that a laundry basket is a tool for laundry that you should revere, otherwise it'll make more work for you.

to maintain. When you take your clothes off, put them in the dang laundry basket. You may have to consciously switch something up to rework this habit if you are a chronic drop-your-clothes-and-run kind of person. One simple idea is switching up where you undress: Do it right next to the laundry basket. By keeping everything in the basket, it takes away the resistance of picking up laundry haphazardly strewn everywhere before beginning a load. Instead, all your clothes are sitting there waiting for their turn to be washed.

This habit is intertwined with staying on top of laundry. There will be times when life happens and for a small stretch of time you get behind on house chores. You'll soon notice when the laundry basket begins overflowing, and it is like a switch turning on. All of a sudden, no one bothers to put their dirty laundry in, on, or sometimes even near the dirty laundry basket.

The Systems

Any laundry system I have figured out over the years has had one unrelenting goal: Make laundry as easy as possible to do. For this section, I'll focus on specific problem-oriented solutions to streamline a laundry room.

Problem: *Laundry Room in Another Zip Code*

My biggest regret in our last home remodel was not putting a washer and dryer upstairs when we completely gutted the house. When I was designing the home, I knew that laundry on a different floor on the opposite end of the house from the bedroom would be less than ideal, but it took living there for me to realize what a monumental pain in the you-know-what it was. If you have a similar laundry setup, I feel your pain. Here are some systems to help make life a bit easier.

- **Get a rolling laundry sorter:** This is a multi-compartment laundry basket on wheels. If your laundry room is on a different level of your home and you have space for it, get one for each floor. This was hands down some of the best money I spent on my home over the years. I had one with four different compartments, and each one could be removed individually and dumped in the washing machine.

- **Bypass the stairs:** If you have mobility issues, a narrow staircase, or are just tired, hauling laundry up and down can put a damper on keeping up with laundry. One option is to tear through the walls and make a cool laundry chute. I was so desperate in our last house I seriously considered this. Another option is to throw your laundry down the stairs. This was my daughter's favorite way to help with laundry in our last house. We'd bring our laundry baskets to the top of the stairs and throw it all over the railing. At the bottom she'd jump into the massive pile of clothes while I sorted the laundry into my rolling hamper.

- **Shift your closets:** Another outside-the-box idea I've seen is having a communal closet where the laundry room is. One viral video I saw showed how one mom made a family closet in the basement by the laundry room. Everyone's clean clothes were put away there, and it was a system that worked well for the whole family.

A system does not have to be conventional to work. The point is this: if stairs are the biggest obstacle between you and clean clothes, I give you permission to figure out a way to eliminate them.

Problem: *Itty-Bitty Living Space*

If your laundry room is more like a laundry corner (or closet), congrats! You will be the best at having successful systems to make your laundry space functional.

- **Streamline your laundry routine:** If you are struggling with storage and space where you do your laundry, it may be time to simplify your routine—including products. Did you know your clothes don't need softener? For real life, it's completely optional. Instead of big jugs of detergent, maybe start using a laundry powder that will fit in a pliable bag and slide into a small space, or play with switching individual things out for products that cover more than one step. Make it as easy as possible to reach for detergent and start a load.

- **Get collapsible laundry baskets:** You can buy laundry baskets that pop out to become a full-size basket and collapse down flat for easy storage. They are a huge help in a tight space.

IF YOU DON'T HAVE A WASHING MACHINE . . .

You are the MVP. If you have to haul laundry back and forth, helpful systems can make all the difference in your laundry routine:

- **Get picky about your laundry bags:** Invest in good quality laundry bags or baskets that are easy to transport and don't allow your freshly cleaned clothes to get dirty.

- **Sort your laundry before you leave home:** You can use a laundry sorter with removable bags and sort your dirty clothes when you are putting them in the basket in the first place to save more work for yourself later.

- **Spot treat your clothes for stains before you leave:** This will give the spot treatment time to work its magic and ensure all your clothes are ready to get tossed straight in the washing machine.

- **Have a laundry bag or backpack ready to go with supplies:** Opt for lighter, leaner laundry supplies so you can bring a little at a time. Keep your laundry bag/backpack stocked and ready to avoid the added step of tracking your supplies down before you head out the door.

- **Utilize help:** If you need or want it, utilize a laundry service that will come pick up your dirty clothes and drop them off clean. If a regular laundry service isn't in the budget, use a hybrid system with a service every once in a while to take the load off your normal laundry routine (pun SO intended).

- **Overschedule your laundry time:** Give yourself extra time when you get home to fold and put away all of your laundry.

- **Hang things up:** If you are like me, the laundry room is also where things like brooms, dusters, cleaning supplies, and the vacuum goes. This can end up being a lot of things to fit in a small area, and when items like these end up sitting on the floor, it can feel cluttered and hard to use (not to mention the tripping hazard). Utilize wall and cabinet space by hanging these items. You can buy "broom grippers" that stick to the wall and are designed to hold a broom handle.

Problem: *More Steps than a Beauty Influencer's Nighttime Skin-Care Routine*

Having an over-complicated laundry routine can create major resistance when it comes to starting and finishing the laundry. Most loads of laundry for me are three steps: Load, a scoop of detergent, and press "Start." Here are some tips to simplify your laundry routine:

THINGS I KEEP WITHIN REACH OF MY WASHING MACHINE

- Detergent
- Oxygen bleach
- Vinegar
- Baking soda
- Lavender dryer sachets
- Washing machine cleaner packets
- Garment bags for delicates

- **Use fewer products:** Even if you have ample storage in the laundry room, having fewer steps to your laundry routine makes it a quicker process for you.

- **Keep everything within reach:** Remove as many barriers to doing your laundry as possible.

- **Find a way to do less:** You can put ALL your colored clothes in with the towels and your undergarments. Find ways to simplify how you wash things so you have less loads and work. Obviously, don't risk ruining your clothes if certain garments need special treatment, but try to simplify the process.

Problem: *Kids in the Mix*

To be clear, kids are *not* a problem. But it does take some problem-solving to find a system that works for and with your kids' laundry.

- **Think outside the dresser box:** When my daughter became old enough to pick out her own clothes, dresser drawers were always open with clothes hanging out everywhere. It took up precious real estate in her room and was always a mess. I switched her dresser out for a cube organizer with storage bins. Now, if a bin doesn't get pushed all the way back in it's not as big of a deal. She can also bring the bins to wherever I'm folding clothes, fill them up, and bring them back to her room.

- **Do you *have* to fold it?** I prefer folded laundry for everyone, and it bothered me when all of my hard work folding would get erased within 2.4 seconds of my kids' clothes being in their drawers. For this stage of my life, I decided to just not care whether my work is undone. I may get to the point where I don't fold my kids' clothes at all if they don't care to keep them folded (because it's not that big of a deal). For now I am still trying. No matter: Don't feel like you have to be constantly refolding your kids' clothes to have them just so. You run this show, you make the rules.

- **Do you *have* to hang it?** When we moved into our new home, we noticed the closet in my son's room has a bunch of shelves and no room for a curtain rod. I thought I'd need to immediately tear all the shelves out and install a rod, but that never happened. If you have a really little one like me, do you have to hang their clothes? Would it be easier to fold the outfits up together in put them in the drawer (or not fold them at all?). Again, you run this show. You get to decide.

- **Teach your kids how to do laundry:** Another viral video idea I loved came from a mom of five. She taught her kids how to do laundry young, and designates a day of the week that each child is responsible for doing their own laundry. It's worth a try, or a variation on this, so that you have some helping hands as soon as possible.

The Tutorials

My Simple Laundry Routine

- **For colors:** Use 1 tablespoon (15 g) of powdered laundry detergent. Wash on cold.

- **For whites:** 1 tablespoon (15 g) of powdered laundry detergent + 2 tablespoons (30 g) oxygen bleach powder. Wash on hot with an extra rinse.

- **For towels:** 1 tablespoon (15 g) of powdered laundry detergent and ¾ cup (204 g) of baking soda. Wash on cold.

- **For a stinky load:** Use this for a load that may or may not have been forgotten wet in the washer: 1 tablespoon (15 g) of powdered laundry detergent + 1 cup (235 ml) of vinegar. Wash on hot.

- **For drying:** I keep a dryer ball in with the clothes. It helps everything dry faster and more uniformly, especially things like towels or sheets. If you use a wool one, it helps soften the clothes, and you can add scent as well. I also keep a sachet of dried lavender in the dryer for a subtle, natural scent. I switch it out when the sachet is getting thin.

See my laundry schedule printout on page 169.

Drying Hacks

If you need to dry something fast, throw it in with a clean, dry towel and set the dryer to hot. If you need to de-wrinkle something, put it in the dryer with an ice cube and set the dryer on hot. It will create a bit of steam and de-wrinkle your clothes quick.

BEST PRACTICES FOR STAINS

- Treat the stain immediately.
- Scrape off/remove any residue.
- Apply stain remover and let it soak for about ten minutes.
- Wash.
- *Never* dry clothes if the stain isn't gone. . . Start over at step one.

DIY All-Purpose Stain Remover Recipe

Mix 1 tablespoon (15 ml) of vinegar and 1 tablespoon (15 ml) of dish soap with 2 cups (475 ml) of cold water. Spray or dab on the stain, then wash it out with cool water.

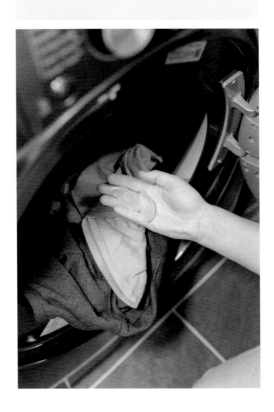

How I Fold Clothes

This folding routine is adapted from the magical Marie Kondo. It saves space, keeps wrinkles at bay, and is super fast once you get the hang of it. Bonus points for being able to see all your clothes when you open your drawer as well!

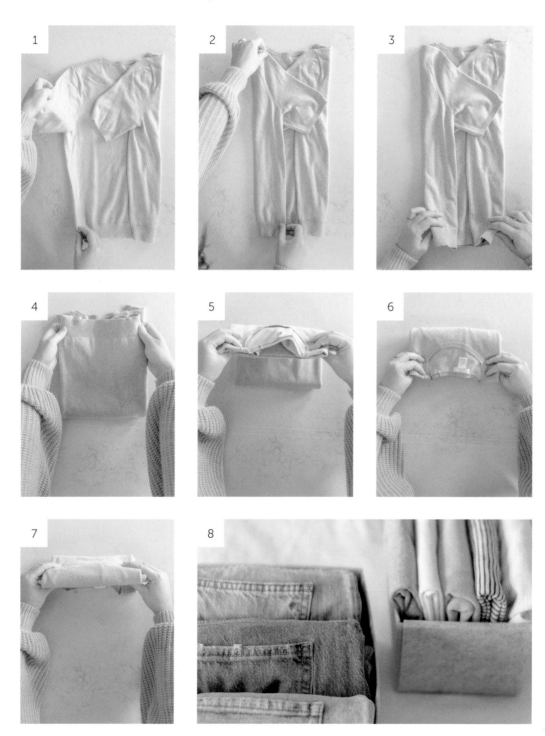

8.

Kids' Spaces

▲▲▲▲▲▲▲▲▲▲▲▲▲▲▲▲▲▲▲▲▲▲▲▲▲▲▲▲▲▲▲▲▲▲▲▲

One morning as I was trying to catch up on dishes, my toddler turned off the washing machine three times, spilled baking soda everywhere (where did he even *get* that?), and got ice out of the freezer, leaving random cubes everywhere to melt. If you are a parent, I don't need to tell you it's a hard gig. And I don't need to spend a single second telling you how impossible it can feel to keep some semblance of order in a household with the sweetest little babies (or big kids) toddling around undoing everything. You and I know it's the best and the hardest and the messiest and the most beautiful way of life.

I do want to take the time to tell you, though, that keeping house with kids doesn't have to exist only on the end of two polar states: the constant stress of keeping everything perfectly tidy with kids or the complete surrender to utter chaos. There can be a spot in the middle, and (you guessed it), I have some systems and habits that I have developed over the years to help you and your kids care more easily for your home.

I have begun to look at the time I spend helping, encouraging, and (admittedly) demanding my children help pick up as a gift. I am giving them the gift of being an important member of the household. I am teaching them to serve others, and I am instilling life skills in them early so the ease into adulthood will be more like riding a bike down a hill with a helmet on and less like a unicycle over a rocky cliff.

The Kids' Space Resets

You will notice that the kids room resets don't follow the exact formula of the resets in the rest of the book. This isn't just about age, although big kids or teenagers can definitely use the bedroom reset. I have found it is helpful to consider the child's age and the way their brain works when setting expectations for them to clean their room. We have had a lot of meltdowns in our house over the years with picking up kids' rooms based on sheer overwhelm. I would say, "Clean your room," and come back an hour later and nothing would really be done. I'd say, "Start by your closet," and the same thing would happen.

After trial and error, my husband and I noticed that with our oldest, it helped if we made a list that divided the room into items (e.g., books, clothes, dolls, etc.). Then she could check things off the list as she went. Working with the way our kids' brains operated, instead of the way we thought things should be done, made the house run a lot more smoothly. The resets in this chapter are designed to take into account different ways your child's brain may be able to handle picking up a messy room. For cute printable versions, see the Appendix (page 165)!

Before having your child reset their room, have a trash bag on hand and a basket to collect things that belong in another room. You can also dedicate a second bag or box to donations.

The Clean Zone Reset

This reset splits the room into zones and has the child clean up each zone. Customize the zones to your child's space.

Step One: Clean up everything in your bed zone. Make your bed.

Step Two: Clean up everything in your closet zone.

Step Three: Clean up everything in your dresser zone.

Step Four: The floor is lava! Clean up everything in the lava zone, making sure you get everything off the floor that doesn't belong!

The Checklist Reset

This reset is more of a straightforward comprehensive list. Of course, customize it to your child's space and belongings!

Step One: Make your bed.

Step Two: Put dirty clothes in the hamper.

Step Three: Hang or put away all clean clothes.

Step Four: Tidy books and put them away.

Step Five: Put toys away.

Step Six: Tidy the tops of bookshelves or dressers.

Step Seven: Look for anything out of place and put it away.

The Cleaning Challenge Reset

Try using the checklist reset as a cleaning challenge. This reset is designed as a game, and it works best when used with the printable "game board" in the Appendix. It is fun to clean up each category and have a celebration at the end. A simple idea is having the child come get a high-five as they check off each item along the game board.

The Color Code Reset

Step One: Clean up anything in your room that is red.

Step Two: Clean up anything in your room that is orange.

Step Three: Clean up anything in your room that is yellow.

Step Four: Clean up anything in your room that is green.

Step Five: Clean up anything in your room that is blue.

Step Six: Clean up anything in your room that is purple.

Step Seven: Clean up anything in your room that is pink.

Step Eight: Clean up anything in your room that is black or gray.

Step Nine: Clean up anything in your room that is brown.

Step Ten: Clean up anything in your room that is white.

Step Eleven: Clean up anything else out of place.

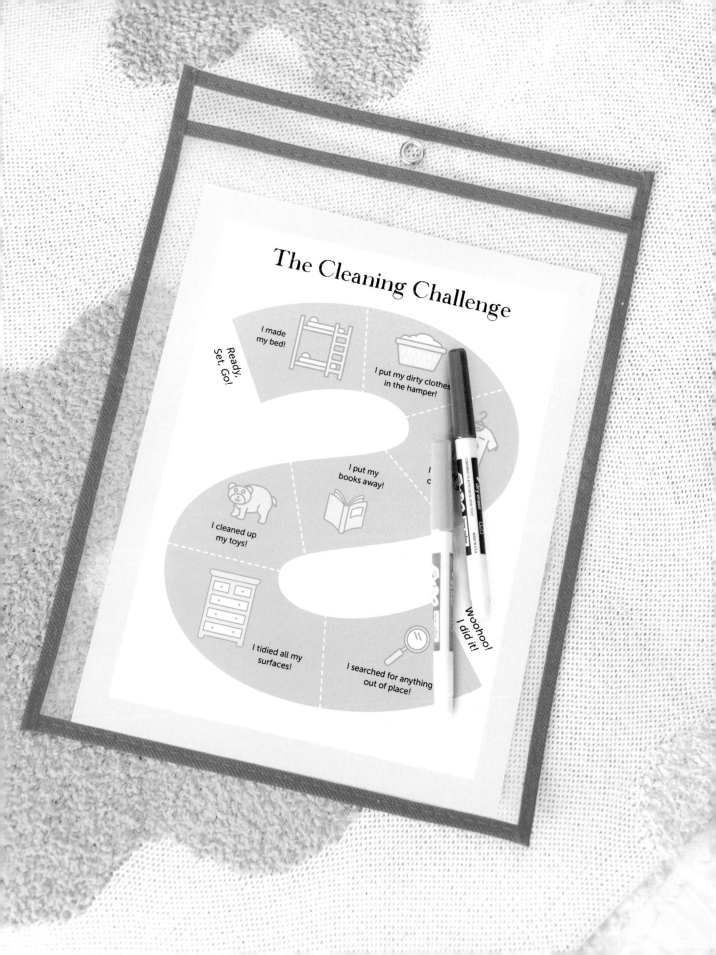

The Habits

At times it feels nearly impossible to change my own habits, so when I think about adding on the task of helping my children change their habits, I feel ready to wave my white flag of surrender. I remember years ago deciding we were going to put every toy back before we moved on to play with the next one. It seemed like a perfect idea—a mom on Instagram said so! I was determined to instill this habit in my three-year-old.

I'm sure you can see the glaring problem much more quickly than it took me to realize. I would have had to do literally nothing else except follow my daughter around and "encourage" (a.k.a. initiate a mini standoff) her to pick up a toy every time she put it down in the middle of playing. It ruined playtime, and it obliterated my goal of having less toys strewn everywhere.

My oldest is ten, and I obviously have *a lot* of parenting still ahead of me, but I have learned some tricks that made instilling better tidiness habits a bit easier:

Make It a Game

Gamifying picking up has worked wonders for my kids, both when they are little and when they get to the bigger kid stage. A lot of these are more imagination focused, as I've found over the years that incorporating some imaginative mission or goal helped my oldest. My favorite ideas for gamifying picking up:

- **Have siblings race each other:** Some good ol' fashioned competition can get kids focused quickly. You can offer a reward ("Whoever finishes first gets to choose a show!") or just let their competitive spirits drive them.

- **Play detective:** Hide something (or several things) in the room that they would have to thoroughly pick up to find. Encourage them to play "detective" and clean up to find the missing item.

- **The floor is lava:** The child obviously has a force field around them, but the toys and clothes strewn about the room don't—and the floor is heating up! Quickly clean up before it is too late!

- **Prepare for an "event":** "We are going to have a tea party or monster truck rally as soon as your room is picked up!"

- **Teach a sibling or stuffy:** Have the child show a sibling or stuff how to clean their room.

- **Celebrate:** Each category picked up earns a dance or a cheer.

Use the Habit Loop

- **Have a fun room cleaning playlist:** A specific playlist for picking up can be a great mental cue for the kids. When that playlist begins, they know it's cleanup time. It may also be helpful for the child to have the same songs play to recognize a beginning and end to their cleaning time.

- **Use a reward to cement the habit loop that is NOT a bribe:** I learned the hard way that it did not work to tell my kids to clean their room "or else" (we won't get to play that, we don't get to do this). Instead, I began to rephrase and use the reward part of the habit loop as something we already would get to do in our day. Some examples: "When you finish cleaning your room, we can play with play dough," "As soon as you're done, it'll be snack time," or "Let's watch a show when you are done cleaning your room!" I found the simple switch in my phrasing worked so much better for our family.

Figure Out What Makes Your Child "Tick"

Parenting is the ultimate game of trial and error. So many ideas I thought were genius and made so much sense were total failures in the parenting department. Keep your chin up, and keep an eye out for ways to help your child instill habits that will help them along throughout life. Some different ways to incorporate habits based on how your child's brain may be receptive to them:

- **Explain why you are asking them to do things a certain way:** For example, we put the toothbrush and toothpaste in the drawer, because it protects them from gross bacteria that flies around the bathroom when we flush the toilet.

- **Use a song or rhyme while you do things:** There is an abundance of cute (or a bit grim, depending on the time period) little rhymes that can help cement things into your child's brain. A quick web search will give you ideas to use or build off of.

- **Use rigid routines:** If you notice your child getting thrown off by a change in routine (e.g., "I can't clean right now. I always have a snack at this time of day!"), use that to your advantage. Incorporate smaller habits throughout the day that work with their normal routines. For example, after their bath and before bedtime stories, straighten all the stuffies so they are ready to read. For bigger kids, use a timer and give them fifteen minutes of dedicated cleanup at a specific time.

- **Hold hands:** For young kids or ones that thrive on closeness and quality time, do a specific chore alongside them, or explain that you will be doing "x" right next to them, while they are doing "z."

Stay Consistent

When I fall off the bandwagon with my tidying habits, the same thing happens to everyone around the house. I set the tone, and I have learned the hard way that consistency is key. Starting over after a break from our regular programming is always a huge battle, but I have noticed that even after a week of consistently drilling habits into our daily routine, my kids begin to thrive and not resist as much, because they know what to expect.

Some good habits to squeeze in each day:

- **Morning bathroom check:** Have everyone check the bathroom simultaneously for anything out of place, especially toothbrushes.

- **Bed making:** This is another habit that everyone can do at the same time.

- **Backpack and lunch box check:** Do this every day after school.

- **Room tidy:** A short and consistent amount of time every day—even fifteen focused minutes—makes a huge difference!

Let Them "Help" from an Early Age

My toddler wants to do everything my husband and I do. When I'm mopping or vacuuming, he gets so excited and just has to join in. This makes the task take five times longer and somehow messier, but most of the time I let him join in. My goal is for cleaning to not be something the kids see mom or dad do, but something that is a normal part of everyday care for their environment.

Focus on Problem Areas First

If you are ready to start incorporating new habits in your day-to-day routine with kids, consider starting with the biggest problem areas first. These could be the everyday frustrating things, that weird smell coming from the kids' room, or things that seem to make the wheels fall off the day.

Narrow down your problem areas to the highest priority habits. For example: Backpacks never get hung up and lunch boxes don't get emptied. Try using the daily act of walking in the door to prompt these helpful habits. When backpacks and lunch boxes are taken care of, take time to celebrate with an after-school snack.

Put Things in Perspective

One day I decided to switch up the narrative with my "reminders" for my kids to take care of things. Instead of asking my daughter to pick something up, I said, "Oh, I noticed you left that out for me to pick up." I was taken aback by how incredibly offended she was while earnestly explaining she does *not* leave things out just for me to pick up. Now I'll use that phrase as a reminder every so often to put things in perspective—because the truth is, if things get left out, the burden falls on me to pick them up.

TO CHART OR NOT TO CHART

Do chore charts work for you? If so, that is amazing. Stick with what works and skip this section. If they don't, read on. As I've mentioned before, being diagnosed with ADHD as an adult shifted my perspective in keeping house—and it *really* shifted my perspective on the way I raise my children.

One of my shifts was chore charts. We had tried so many times, and after using it for a day it's like the chore chart did not even exist. I realized the reason chore charts weren't working wasn't because I was a crummy, undisciplined mom. I realized it was a tool that did not fit in my tool belt. I kept trying to fit what I thought should go in there and getting exasperated when those tools didn't work for me.

If you cannot keep up with chore charts, focus on habits, one at a time. Use those small habits to piggyback on bigger ones, and soon you'll realize that the chore chart becomes obsolete—and somehow magically everything you had wanted to get done does.

The Systems

Easy Storage

Over the years I've realized if my systems are too complicated, they won't get used. This is especially true with my children, so I've tried to make every storage and tidying system as simple and efficient as possible. These are the storage systems we use at home to make keeping things tidy easier:

- **Clothing bins:** The drawers in the dresser in my eldest's room would fall out if opened a bit too far, and they were impossible to get back in. For a little one, this meant drawers full of clothes constantly on the floor or halfway out of the dresser. We moved to a cube organizer with square fabric storage cubes to hold clothes. She can easily push the cubes back in if they come out, and she can bring them to me when I'm folding her laundry and put her clothes away immediately. My youngest has a dresser with large drawers that are easy to open and close (and stay in). I use cloth boxes in the drawers to separate the little clothes into categories that make putting laundry away and finding new jammies in a dark room easy.

- **Towel hooks:** Towel bars are so hard with kids. They make your towels look lovely and help towels dry quickly, but what kid is going to consistently fold and hang towels nicely on the bar? I'm sure there are some, but they don't live in my house! Towel hooks are a great easy-to-use system that will get your kids hanging their towels more often.

- **Designated drawers:** I tend to put child locks on *everything* I can. Not because every cabinet or drawer has something dangerous to my kids, but because I really don't like cleaning up unnecessary messes. My youngest has a designated drawer with his plates, cups, and bowls. He loves getting his plate out for meals and helping empty the dishwasher by putting his dishes away. Everything else is pretty much locked away until we get out of the toddler stage, because I have turned around to discover flour or rice all over the kitchen floor one too many times over the years.

- **Shoe basket:** Keeping a basket by the door is my low-tech high-results shoe storage solution. There is nothing groundbreaking about this tip, but finding a system that your kids will actually use makes life so much easier—and less of a trip hazard!

- **Folding systems:** As I mentioned in the laundry chapter, you do not have to fold clothes. I have a bit of a hybrid system: For my youngest, I don't fold jammies or one-piece play outfits, but I do fold the rest so I can see clothes quickly when I open the drawer. I fold my eldest's clothes, and then I don't worry about whether she keeps them folded or not.

Less Is More

I often think about the difference in the number of toys between my firstborn and second-born, and I cringe. As the first grandchild on both sides with a large extended family, she accumulated more toys than any child would ever need in her first few years of life. With our second, we have been much more intentional with what we buy and allow or request for gifts. His room and our house are much more manageable at the toddler stage than it was with my oldest at the same age.

I also can't help but notice that when my kids have had less options to play with, they are more content, calm, and play with the toys for longer periods of time.

Toy Rotation

There is a whole subsection of mom culture that shares toy rotation content. Weekly or biweekly they reset their kids' rooms or playroom with different toys, often setting them up beautifully. You don't have to spend hours each week to make this concept work for you. Whether you want to do the social media–worthy rotation or just make toy management a bit easier, here are some toy rotation tips to adapt to your routine:

- **Clear bins with lids:** In the early-elementary years, my daughter had so many different types of toys she loved to play with. She had Barbie dolls, baby dolls, dress up, horses, and princesses that were all played with separately. Throwing them all in a toy box wasn't working, and keeping them all out on the floor at once *really* wasn't working. I ended up getting small, inexpensive clear stackable totes with lids and labeling them with each category of toy. I made sure the bins fit under my daughter's bed and in her closet so she could put them away herself. This has been such a helpful hack. It simultaneously makes it easier to find and get out toys while more difficult to get everything out and make messes.

- **Closet storage:** You can also use the bin storage system to rotate toys. Store playsets in separate bins and keep them in a closet. Get one bin out for the week and switch to a new one the next week. I noticed that my toddler played with his toys with much more concentration when I do this—and it really helps with mess!

Bedding

Making your bed is such a great way to set the tone for the day. When my daughter was ready for her big girl bed, I made it so cute. There was a comforter and coordinating duvet folded nicely at the end of the bed, with the fancy pillow sham sitting perfectly in front of her sleeping pillow and a sweet little stuffy (she cared nothing about) resting angelically on them. The only problem was it never *ever* looked like that again. My four-year-old was neither capable of nor cared about the fancy bed setup I had concocted.

Don't be like me and make it impossible for your kids to make their beds nicely. These hacks can eliminate resistance for you and your kids when it comes to making their bed and keeping it nice:

- **Zippered bedding:** Once you try this, you will never look back. You can buy bedding that zips up! Like the comfiest, softest sleeping bag you've ever used, a zippered bed set looks like a made bed with a comforter and sheet but zips up along the sides and bottom. They are easy to clean and put on the beds and make it so your kids can actually make their bed. Bonus: The comforter won't slide off, leaving a cold kid every night.

- **Waterproof mattress pad:** This is a must-have for cribs and big kid beds (and any bed, really). Using a waterproof mattress pad will save your mattress more than once over the years. Being able to strip down sheets and the mattress pad in the middle of the night with a sick child and having a clean and dry mattress underneath is a lifesaver. I know a lot of seasoned moms that use multiple layers of mattress pads and sheets on cribs so that they can take off one layer and have the next already on the mattress ready to go in the night.

- **Simplified system:** Remember the acronym KISS? Keep it simple, stupid. You're not stupid. You're really smart and amazing. But sometimes it is stupid how much we complicate things for our kids (okay, maybe just me). If it makes you smile, remind yourself "KISS" when setting up your kid's bed and room.

Bath Time

I think my family's ability to destroy a bathroom in a single nightly bath-time routine qualifies as a superpower. Water, clothes, dishes, and random toys are stranded everywhere. The walls are splashed with water and hair product. The floor is a mine field of bath toys.

If you are like me, bath time before bed is an integral part of winding down for the night (and keeping mom's sanity intact). However, when the bathroom gets destroyed during the process, I certainly don't feel more calm and ready for bed. I have developed some systems over the years to keep the bathroom more or less intact after the bath or shower routine, and most revolve around my bedding philosophy (KISS).

- **Fewer doohickies:** There are *so many* cool doohickies, gadgets, and thingamabobs marketed to make your kid's bath time more fun. The only problem with all this bath time fun is how not fun it is to keep track of and clean up. That, and the fact that once we are in the new-toy-constantly cycle it is hard to get out of. We don't own bath toys anymore. I'll let my kids grab a couple of water-safe toys from their rooms (they go back in their rooms when they are dry), or keep a toy or two on the edge of the bath.

- **Smart storage:** You can get a plastic basket with handles and holes in the side in any color at the dollar store. It's easy to toss bath toys into and will let water drain out. You can add rust-free metal shower shelves to store shampoo for the whole family that sticks right to the wall. Pick bathroom storage that is easy to use and not cumbersome.

- **Soap solutions:** My second-born had terrible eczema when he was an infant. Through trying to figure out how to help his poor little body, we discovered how little soap we actually need to use. Surprisingly, the bathtub and shower stayed cleaner the less soap (and the more basic ingredient lists) we used. Think through what you use for hygiene items and decide if the number of bottles you tidy is worth it, along with the residue they may leave in the bath. A prime example: my husband's affinity for dark blue soap. It smells great, but is a pain to clean out of the grout.

The Tutorials

How to Clean Common Kid Messes

- **Sharpie:** For fabric, dab with rubbing alcohol, then rinse with cool water. Repeat until the stain lifts. For well-lacquered furniture, finished wood, or windows, use rubbing alcohol on a cotton pad to wipe the stain off. You can also wet a melamine sponge and wipe it down. For furniture, always test an inconspicuous area first with the rubbing alcohol or melamine sponge to make sure you don't ruin the paint or finish.

- **Wall smudges:** Use a melamine sponge or damp cloth with a dab of dish soap. A melamine sponge works well for crayon or washable marker on the walls as well.

- **Grass, berry, or juice stain:** Mix one part distilled white vinegar and one part water. Pour or spray onto the stain and let it sit. Wash in cool water. Repeat until the stain is gone. Do not dry until stain is lifted!

> ### REMOVE A MATTRESS STAIN
>
> Generously spray the stain with one part distilled white vinegar and one part Water Let it sit for fifteen minutes. Blot with a clean rag or paper towels to lift the stain and moisture, then sprinkle with baking soda. Let the baking soda sit for at least five hours, then vacuum it up.

- **Sickies:** On a mattress, follow the steps for removing stains to clean up as much of the mess as possible. On furniture or carpet, clean up the chunks first. (Cringe, sorry. We've all been here.) Then, if you have a portable upholstery cleaner, use it with the solution. If not, clean up as much of the mess as possible, leaving only the stain. Use kitchen utensils to scoop it out of carpet fibers if needed. Use upholstery or carpet cleaner or a mixture of 2 cups (475 ml) of water to 1 cup (235 ml) of vinegar with a teaspoon of clear dish soap. Blot the stain with a clean rag or gently scrub it with a soft-bristled cleaning brush, rinsing the rag or brush periodically. Blot with a clean, dry rag to lift the stain, and repeat until the stain is gone.

Checklists

Example Morning Checklist

- ◯ Empty the dishwasher and clean up the breakfast dishes.
- ◯ Brush your teeth. Put away your toothbrush and toothpaste.
- ◯ Put your jammies in the laundry basket or drawer.
- ◯ Make your bed.
- ◯ Put your shoes away nicely.

Example Before Bed Checklist

- ◯ Hang up your towel in the bathroom.
- ◯ Brush your teeth. Put the toothpaste and your toothbrush away.
- ◯ Put your dirty clothes in the basket.
- ◯ Pick up your toys.
- ◯ Set out clothes for tomorrow.

Appendix

Reset Rotations

Every room reset is designed for you to incorporate into your routine however you'd like. That being said, I know a lot of people like specifics and concrete ideas to work with. Here are some ways to use the resets in a rotation to get to the whole house. Because we all operate differently, I have sample Reset Rotations to get to the whole house weekly, biweekly, or monthly. Feel free to come up with your own additions.

If you like to stay in the habit of taking the time every day to completely reset a room, the weekly reset rotation probably would be a great fit. If you are a weekend cleaning warrior or like to squeeze resets in throughout the week, the biweekly rotation may work great for you. If you like to spread out your cleaning, or if you currently need to dedicate more time and energy to other things, or if you have occasional help, the monthly reset rotation could be just what you need.

Weekly Reset Rotation

As a reminder: Make these your own!! I like to start the week off with my least favorite reset, but easing into the week with the easiest or your favorite room to reset may be more your style.

Everyday Tasks

○ Make the bed.

○ Empty and load the dishwasher.

○ Do a fifteen-minute Random Roundup (page 50).

○ Do a quick nightly kitchen reset (page 30).

○ Clear bathroom countertops.

○ Do a load of laundry.

○ File the mail.

MONDAY: Bathrooms

TUESDAY: Bedrooms

WEDNESDAY: Entry spaces and laundry room

THURSDAY: Kitchen and dining

FRIDAY: Living and kids' spaces (living room, bonus room, play room, etc.)

SATURDAY: Catch-up day

SUNDAY: Rest/day off

Biweekly Reset Rotation

Everyday Tasks

○ Make the bed.

○ Empty and load the dishwasher.

○ Do a fifteen-minute Random Roundup (page 50).

○ Do a quick nightly kitchen reset (page 30).

○ Clear the bathroom countertops.

○ Do a load of laundry.

○ File the mail.

WEEK ONE: Bathrooms, bedrooms, kids' spaces, entryway

WEEK TWO: Laundry room, kitchen and dining, living spaces

Monthly Reset Rotations

I have made two examples of monthly rotations. The first one hits the areas that need the most TLC germ-wise (the bathroom and the kitchen) every other week, while spreading out the rest of the house accordingly. One option for the monthly rotations also is to spread out the bathrooms on different weeks if you have multiple and that sounds more feasible (e.g., week one master bathroom, week three kids' and guest bathroom).

Monthly Reset Rotation A
Everyday Tasks

○ Make the bed.

○ Empty and load the dishwasher

○ Do a fifteen-minute Random Roundup (page 50).

○ Do a quick nightly kitchen reset (page 30).

○ Clear the bathroom countertops.

○ Do a load of laundry.

○ File mail.

WEEK ONE: Bathroom, bedrooms
WEEK TWO: Kitchen, dining, entry spaces
WEEK THREE: Bathroom, laundry room
WEEK FOUR: Kitchen, kids' spaces, catch up

Monthly Reset Rotation B
Everyday Tasks

○ Make the bed.

○ Empty and load dishwasher.

○ Do a fifteen-minute Random Roundup (page 50).

○ Do a quick nightly kitchen reset (page 30).

○ Clear the bathroom countertops.

○ Do a load of laundry.

○ File the mail.

WEEK ONE: Bathrooms, bedrooms
WEEK TWO: Kitchen and dining
WEEK THREE: Laundry room, kids' spaces
WEEK FOUR: Entry spaces, catch-up week

Seasonal Resets

Fall

- Clean the gutters.
- Clean any outdoor furniture.
- Store away summer clothes and seasonal items.
- Change the furnace filter.
- Check the fireplace for needed maintenance.
- Check and clean the dryer vent.
- Deep clean the kitchen.

Winter

- Get out and organize the winter clothing and activity items.
- Clean the carpets.
- Put away Christmas or holiday décor and store until next year.
- Put out heavy-duty rugs for wet boots and clothes.
- Reverse ceiling fans (to counter-clockwise).
- Change the furnace filter.
- Wash the curtains or drapes.
- Deep clean the laundry and entryway spaces.

Spring

- Wash the rugs.
- Wash the windows and door screens.
- Wash outdoor toys.
- Air out the house
- Store away winter clothes and seasonal items.
- Begin pest control.
- Change the furnace filter.
- Deep clean the kids' rooms and spaces.

Summer

- Reverse the ceiling fans (to clockwise).
- Power wash porches/decks and garage.
- Clean any outdoor furniture.
- Deep clean the bedrooms, closets, and living areas.
- Do any heavy dusting as needed.
- Vacuum and spot clean the furniture.
- Change the furnace filter.

Printables

Scan this QR code to download the following printables.

The Cleaning Challenge

Ready,
Set, Go!

I made
my bed!

I put my dirty clothes
in the hamper!

I put my clean
clothes away!

I put my
books away!

I cleaned up
my toys!

I tidied all my
surfaces!

I searched for anything
out of place!

Woohoo!
I did it!

Clean Zone Checklist

Bed Zone

Closet Zone

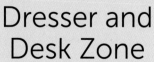

Dresser and
Desk Zone

Lava Zone

Room Cleaning Checklist

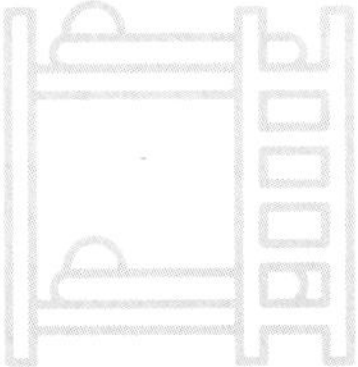

- [ ] Bed made
- [ ] Dirty clothes in hamper
- [ ] Clean clothes put away 
- [ ] Books tided and put away 
- [ ] Toys put away 
- [ ] Surfaces tidied 
- [ ] Anything out of place tidied and put away

The Keeping Home List

Morning	Evening

Throughout the day

_____   _____

_____   _____

_____   _____

WEEKLY SCHEDULE

Monday	Tuesday	Wednesday	Friday	Saturday	Sunday

On-Track Tasks

_____   _____

_____   _____

_____   _____

Laundry Schedule

Monday	Bedding
Tuesday	Colors
Wednesday	Towels
Thursday	Colors
Friday	Whites
Saturday	Catch Up
Sunday	Rest

Citations

Chapter One
Clear, James. *Atomic Habits*. New York: Random House, 2018.

Duhigg, Charles. *The Power of Habit: Why We Do What We Do in Life and Business*. 10th anniversary edition. New York: Random House Trade Paperbacks, 2023.

Pressfield, Steven. *The War of Art: Break through the Blocks and Win Your Inner Creative Battles*. Black Irish Entertainment LLC, 2002.

Chapter Two
Curran, E. J. "7 Science-Based Benefits of Eating Together as a Family." *Parents*, February 13, 2023. https://www.parents.com/recipes/tips/unexpected-benefits-of-eating-together-as-a-family-according-to-science/.

Resources

My website: karissaathome.com

Books on Habits That Have Shaped Me

Clear, James. *Atomic Habits*. New York: Avery, 2018.

Duhigg, Charles. *The Power of Habit: Why We Do What We Do in Life and Business*. 10th anniversary edition. New York: Random House Trade Paperbacks, 2023.

Earley, Justin Whitmel. *Habits of the Household: Practicing the Story of God in Everyday Family Rhythms*. Grand Rapids: Zondervan, 2021.

Pressfield, Steven. *The War of Art: Break through the Blocks and Win Your Inner Creative Battles*. Black Irish Entertainment LLC, 2002.

Home Books That Have Shaped Me

Postel-Vinay, Danielle. *Home Sweet Maison: The French Art of Making a Home*. New York: HarperCollins, 2018.

Shearer, Clea and Joanna Teplin. *The Home Edit: A Guide to Organizing and Realizing Your House Goals*. New York: Clarkson Potter, 2019.

Smith, Myquillyn. *Cozy Minimalist Home: More Style, Less Stuff*. Grand Rapids: Zondervan, 2018.

Dedication

To my mom for making our home, my dad for building it up, and my husband for being it. Lastly, to my children, for giving me the world.

Acknowledgments

"I have learned to kiss the wave that has thrown me against the Rock of Ages."

—Charles Spurgeon

I have been tossed about by my share of waves in the short time I've been on earth, and have always found refuge in the great I Am. I am so thankful to God for the abundance of blessings, but I must thank Him as well for my weaknesses. May I boast all the more gladly of them, for in my weakness I find my strength in Him.

I have been one of those fortunate enough to have found love early and gotten to grow up alongside my best friend. Colin, I could not be more proud of the man you are, or more thankful to be married to you. You have been my biggest cheerleader and supporter as I take on this new adventure, and I'm so grateful. What a life so far, huh?!

My children have been such a joy through the ups and downs of the past several years, including the year that we took on another remodel at the same time mom decided to write a book. Caroline, I am so proud of you in every way. You are magnificent. Thank you for being proud of me in return and excited for me as I wrote this book. You kept me going even when I wanted to give up! Gideon, you, sweet boy, were the most blessed distraction to the stress of finishing this book. I could always count on you to make me smile or ask for a snuggle when I needed a break.

My parents have been a constant support in our lives, graciously loving us through every season. Mom, thank you for fighting for your kids in every meaningful way every day of motherhood and for your selfless love. We are all infinitely better off because of you. Dad, some of my greatest memories throughout my entire life have been doing things alongside you. Thank you for that gift, and every other you have given me—tangible or otherwise.

Uncle Dave, seeing you be excited over this opportunity for me and being proud of me filled my heart to the brim. Thanks for getting me all set to write and cheering me on. You mean the world to me.

I am ever so grateful to my in-laws, Dock and Jen. What wonderful people you are. I am so glad to be "yours," and that you have always accepted me as I am (messy house and all!). Thank you for always supporting us.

There are so many more people to thank for this opportunity and for bringing this book to fruition. It really begins with my editor Thom O'Hearn. Thank you for taking a chance on me. Your kindness, wisdom, guidance, and support through this whole process has somehow made writing this book one of the least stressful parts of life currently. I will be forever grateful to you and the entire hardworking team at Quarto for this opportunity!

To my talented art director Hailey Toohey and amazing photographer Oxana Brik. Thank you for making this book beautiful! You helped me branch way out of my comfort zone, and working with both of you was such a pleasure and amazing experience.

A special thanks to Pete Taylor. I know how valuable your time is, and for you to give me a precious amount to help me navigate this strange career is something I will always be grateful for. Derek Wolf, what a kindness you gave me through the introduction to Thom. Thank you!

Our contractor Dan Wilcott also deserves a huge shoutout. He worked tirelessly to remodel our house just in the nick of time for each photo shoot. Definitely not what you signed up for Dan, but you went above and beyond. Colin and I are so grateful!

Lastly, the audience that has tagged along with every remodel, reset, and cleaning hack. This book would not exist without you or your kind support. Thank you, from the bottom of my heart.

About the Author

Tired of being inundated with curated, picture-perfect displays of homemaking that were completely unrelatable, **Karissa Barker** set out to blog with a mission. She would design her attainable content to give a new generation of homemakers the know-how needed to run a household their way. Recognizing that most people have no idea what they are doing when it comes to designing, organizing, and the upkeep of a home, Karissa built her brand on teaching solid, achievable basics. Today, she has expanded to about a million followers across TikTok, Instagram, and YouTube, but she still maintains her blog, newsletter, and storefront at karissaathome.com.

Index